DORSET

CURIOUS AND SURPRISING

DORSET
CURIOUS AND SURPRISING

ROGER GUTTRIDGE

HALSGROVE

First published in Great Britain in 2016

British Library Cataloguing-in-Publication Data
A CIP record for this title is available from the British Library

ISBN 978 0 85704 297 2

HALSGROVE
Halsgrove House,
Ryelands Business Park,
Bagley Road, Wellington, Somerset TA21 9PZ
Tel: 01823 653777   Fax: 01823 216796
email: sales@halsgrove.com

Part of the Halsgrove group of companies
Information on all Halsgrove titles is available at: www.halsgrove.com

Printed in the UK by T J International

Contents

Acknowledgements

Many of the tales in this volume are drawn from stories I have written for various Dorset newpapers, magazines and book publishers over the last forty years or so and I gratefully acknowledge those who have supplied information and/or pictures. Where appropriate, I have also acknowledged them by quoting them in the text. I am also pleased to acknowledge those who have helped more directly and more recently, including Lady Caroline Conran; Steve Burden; John Tory; Anthony and Rachel Rich; Rosemary Ellerbeck; Jan Ridout; Jane Ferentzi-Sheppard; Imogen Bittner, curator, Sturminster Newton Museum; Jocelyn and Eric Vining; Annika Tallo of Tallin, Estonia; Harriet Chase, general manager of the World's End, Almer; and my wife, Sylvie, for taking many of the photographs.

CHAPTER ONE

The Skeleton in Mary's Cupboard

The macabre story that unfolded at Wimborne in 1913 had its beginnings three years earlier, when neighbours noticed a putrid smell emanating from a cottage in Station Terrace. The stench was the talk of the neighbourhood in the summer of 1910 but it was not until February 1913 that its cause came to light – and when it finally did, it made headlines across the land.

'Lived for years with a skeleton,' declared one newspaper.

'Woman's sacrifice for fear of being haunted,' said another.

At the centre of the story were two elderly spinsters, who shared the cottage at 15 Station Terrace, within a stone's throw of both Wimborne railway station and the town's livestock market. Mary Sarah Kearley and Ellen Griffin – known as Nelly – had first met more than thirty years earlier, when they lived and worked as servants in the same London house. They became devoted friends and, after saving their hard-earned cash for years, spent £100 on a house at Paddington intending to take in boarders. But the venture was a disaster. The boarders never came and the ladies were eventually forced to sell their furniture to pay their debts. Broke and broken-hearted, they left London for Wimborne, where Mary – daughter of the late Josiah Kearley, of Lodge Hill, Holt – was born and brought up.

They lived at Colehill for a while before moving to Station Terrace in 1902. Here for the next few years they lived a fairly reclusive existence, surviving on Mary's modest earnings as a housekeeper at Colehill and a cleaner in Lord Wimborne's Nineveh gallery of Assyrian antiquities at Canford Manor. The ladies were rarely seen in public. In fact Nelly was never seen after about 1905 or 1906, although Mary occasionally assured inquiring neighbours that her companion was 'much better' and 'quite happy'.

Artist's sketch of Mary Kearley arriving at the inquest

The cottage at 15 Station Terrace in 1913

'Miss Kearley spoke very highly of her friend Nelly, and appeared very devoted to her,' said neighbour Mrs Cole, who lived next door. She added that it was understood that Miss Griffin preferred to live as a recluse, so her absence for years on end caused no great surprise.

The truth about Nelly only began to emerge when the Wimborne Urban District Council surveyor, Charles Munckton, had to carry out an inspection of the house under the provisions of a new Housing Act. Several times his knocks went unanswered and when he finally did find Sarah Kearley at home, she refused to let him go upstairs and became quite upset.

'She told him that her "friend" was very much upset by someone knocking at the door the night before and that it would be better if he called again,' reported the *Daily Express*.

After another unsuccessful visit, Munckton returned with a policeman, Sgt Andrews. They borrowed a ladder and tried to look through the rear bedroom window but it had been whitewashed. There was also a screen between the window and the bed. They eventually broke into the cottage, lit a candle and went upstairs. The sight that awaited them in the back bedroom horrified both men. Pulling back a dark sheet on the bed, Sgt Andrews uncovered a pile of rags and beneath them a complete skeleton.

'Apparently every particle of flesh had disappeared, and it was evident that death must have taken place a long time ago, probably three or four years,' reported the *Western Gazette*.

In a colourful style of journalism that would probably be considered distasteful today, the *Daily Express* added: 'It was as clean a skeleton as the one that Long John Silver and his pirate friends found at the foot of the tree on Spy Glass Hill.'

In her evidence at the subsequent inquest, Mary Kearley explained that Nelly had a weak heart and had died two or three years earlier. Her age then would have been about sixty-four.

'She died about 6 o'clock in the morning. I found her dying and gave her some rum,' said Mary, who was two or three years younger than her companion. 'I stayed with her about half-an-hour, when she fainted away and died. I left to go to work at Canford House. I did not tell anyone. I had talked over the matter with her and she expressed a wish to be buried at Richmond [Surrey]. I was to keep her as long as I lived so we could be buried together. She threatened that if she was buried in a churchyard or cemetery, she would haunt me afterwards.'

According to one newspaper, Nelly had a particular dislike of Wimborne Cemetery.

'Did you believe she would haunt you?' asked the coroner in surprise.

'Yes,' replied Mary in a whisper.

She added that she had slept alongside her companion for the first two nights after she died.

'What good purpose could it serve?' asked the coroner.

'I thought she might come to life again,' Mary replied.

Had she moved house, she said, she would have put the bones in a box and taken them with her so she could keep her word.

There were many surreal moments during the inquest, not least when Mary Kearley smiled at the coroner and announced: 'My mother used to be your nurse.'

'Yes, yes, I know,' he replied. 'But we want to hear about Miss Griffin.'

The inquest jury returned an open verdict. Mary Kearley was charged with failing to report a death and remanded in custody. The outcome of the case is unknown.

'The police say they would not keep her in a cell if they could help it,' one national newspaper concluded. 'But little Miss Kearley

Police escort Mary Kearley to the inquest

has no friends, not even the dead one now, and has nowhere to go. But she kept her word.'

The story kept Wimborne's gossips going for months. But the following year the First World War broke out. The inhabitants had other things on their minds and the sensational events of 1913 slipped out of local folklore for almost 100 years. It was not until 2009, when someone donated an album of newspaper cuttings to the Priest's House Museum at Wimborne, that the extraordinary tale came to light once again.

CHAPTER TWO
Puddletown's Royal Secret

For almost three decades in the early nineteenth century, the walls of a grand old manor house in the heart of Dorset guarded a secret that would have scandalised the royal family. It was only in 1829, when the adopted son of the squire of Ilsington House at Puddletown claimed his royal birthright, that the story became public for the first time. It was a tale that had its beginnings at Windsor Castle thirty years earlier and at Weymouth nine months after that – although those beginnings remain shrouded in mystery even today.

At the centre of events was Princess

Princess Sophia

Sophia, the fifth of King George III's six daughters. Born on 5 November 1777, Sophia was a delicate child but also a popular one within royal circles. 'Not only was she sensitive, witty and warm-hearted, mercurial, unexpected and humorous, but she was beautiful,' says her biographer, Lucille Iremonger. 'She was kind. She was seductive. She was very intelligent – and she was universally loved. In short, she was enchanting.'

But she was also a victim of the King's repression. Sophia's obsessively protective father denied her and her sisters the right to move freely in society and barred them from marrying men of their choice under the Royal Marriage Act of 1778. Despite George's best efforts, however, the princesses were occasionally able to enjoy romantic liaisons with the men of the royal household at Windsor – secretly, of course. And Sophia was no exception.

It must have been close to or even on her 22nd birthday that Princess Sophia became pregnant. Nine months later, on 5 August 1800, she gave birth to a son in the Dorset resort of Weymouth, where the royal family were as usual spending the summer season at Gloucester Lodge. News of both pregnancy and birth were kept from the King, who was told his daughter had dropsy, a painful accumulation of fluid beneath the skin. When, after 5 August, she made a spectacular recovery, the King was told she had been cured by 'eating roast beef'. He often told people about this, commenting that it was a 'very extraordinary thing'.

But there were some in the royal court who needed to know the truth and did. 'Arrangements' had to be made for the pregnant Sophia and her child and these provided ample fodder for the gossips of the day. A Weymouth tailor's wife called Sharland, who was expecting a baby at about the same time, had a surprise visit from the princess's doctor. After delivering the first baby, a boy, the midwife attending Mrs Sharland was told by the doctor to leave for a while and come back later. When she returned, there were two babies and she was informed that in her absence Mrs Sharland had given birth to a second boy, twin brother of the first. The midwife was highly sceptical and questioned Mrs Sharland. The new mum eventually revealed that the second baby had been brought in from a carriage and placed by her side with a purse of money and instructions that 'she must say it was her own'. The midwife was under no obligation to keep the secret. And she did not.

The boy was baptised at St Mary's, Melcombe Regis, less than two weeks later. The entry in the parish register reads: 'Thomas Ward, a stranger, adopted by Samuel and Charlotte Sharland. Born 5 August 1800. Baptised 14 August 1800.' Intriguingly, a second entry appears in December 1802 recording the baptism of Thomas Ward, son of Samuel and Charlotte Sharland. It has been suggested that those ultimately responsible for Thomas's welfare were unaware of the original baptism and did not wish to draw attention to it by asking if it had already taken place.

The infant spent at least his first two years with the Sharlands, whose family business prospered. Many were the nobles and gentlemen who arrived to order a new suit, a riding-habit or some other garment while really intent on satisfying their curiosity concerning the new arrival. The child may have remained with the Sharlands indefinitely had not the tailor 'gone about everywhere boasting about the great charge committed to his care'. The final straw was his visit to Major General Thomas Garth, of Stinsford, the King's principal equerry and the supplier of funds for the child's maintenance. Mr Sharland wanted to know the identity of the boy's real parents 'that he might consult directly with them respecting its welfare'. The boy was promptly removed from Mrs Sharland's care and taken to General Garth's house, where an army sergeant's wife was hired to nurse him. When the sergeant was posted overseas, and his wife went with him, the child acquired his third foster-mother at Puddletown, where General Garth was now living at Ilsington House.

It was a house fit for a princess's son. Built in 1690 by the seventh Earl of Huntingdon on the site of a Norman hunting lodge, its main hall was copied directly from the Queen's Entrance at Kensington Palace, designed by Hawksmoor and Wren. The hall has three-quarter-inch-thick oak panelling, discovered some years ago, when layers of Victorian varnish and other decor were stripped off for redecoration. Owners have included the Earls of Orford, the first of whom, the son of England's first Prime Minister, Sir Robert Walpole, was granted the estate as a dowry when he married Baroness Clinton and Treffusis in 1723.

By royal command, the house was leased from 1780-1830 to General Garth, who used to ride to Weymouth and back twice a day when the royal family were at Gloucester Lodge. Several of George III's 15 children stayed at Ilsington, usually as the final overnight stop on the annual journey to Weymouth. Later visitors included King Edward VII, who stayed there during a shooting trip, and the novelist Thomas Hardy and his wife, Florence, who lunched at Ilsington in 1914.

Tom Garth, as the child became known, was brought up at Puddletown and educated at Harrow. In adult life he ran up huge debts, then used papers

Tommy Garth

apparently identifying his natural father to have his debts paid off and to receive an impressive allowance of £3000 a year. The story appeared in the newspapers in some detail in 1829 but the identity of Tom Garth's father was never revealed. Garth went to live in Yorkshire, married and fathered a daughter.

Many suspected that General Garth was his real father. It was claimed that Garth was alone with Sophia at Windsor Castle's Upper Lodge nine months before the birth. In fact, he had a bedroom directly above hers at a time when the King and Queen were in London and the other princesses were living at Lower Lodge. Lady Caroline Thynne, daughter of the Marquess of Bath, claimed that Sophia was 'so violently in love' with Garth that 'everybody saw it' and she 'could not contain herself in his presence'.

It was also rumoured that the General – more than thirty years older than Princess Sophia – had married her in secret, although officially she remained a spinster for the rest of her seventy-one years. It has even been suggested that the boy's original surname of Ward was a clever variant of Garth, the letters 'gu' and 'w' being etymologically interchangeable, as in 'guardian' and 'warden', 'guarantee' and 'warranty', 'gauge' and 'wage'.

Describing General Garth as a 'very plain man with an ugly claret mark on his face', Lord Glenbervie, who was well placed to pick up royal gossip, wrote in his journal in 1804: 'It is now said the Queen knows the child to be the Princess Sophia's, but that the King does not, but that the Queen thinks Garth the father.' Six years later, however, Lord Glenbervie wrote that the now nine-year-old Tom looked 'most strikingly like the royal family'. General Garth himself once described the boy in a letter as his 'protégé' rather than his son.

But there is a second candidate for the parentage – the widely despised Ernest, Duke of Cumberland, one of Princess Sophia's brothers, later to become King Ernest Augustus I of Hanover. The royal siblings were often seen together in Weymouth, she leaning on his arm, and once he was seen to dart on to the royal yacht, seize the princess and kiss her. Another time they paused to gaze at a child brought to the door by Charlotte Sharland as they passed her house. Tommy Garth's daughter refused to marry, and it was said that she made her decision after learning that her grandparents may have been brother and sister. When the story first appeared in the newspapers in 1829 following Tommy Garth's threat to make his parentage public, one or two editors openly hinted at Cumberland's involvement.

Of Princess Sophia, Lord Glenbervie wrote in 1810 that 'if a sinner, [she] has the demeanour of a very humble and repentant one. She has something very attentive and kind and even affectionate in her demeanour.' There is some evidence that she was visited at Kensington Palace from time to time by her son. Princess Sophia eventually went blind, died in 1848 and was privately buried at Kensal Green.

CHAPTER THREE

The Execution of Martha Brown

It's one of the most famous endings in English literature – the arrest of the sleeping Tess at Stonehenge and the subsequent raising of a black flag from the prison tower as her grief-stricken husband, Angel Clare, and her sister, 'Liza-Lu, mark the moment of her execution nearby. But few of the millions who have read *Tess of the d'Urbervilles* know of the real-life drama that inspired this most heartbreaking of Thomas Hardy tales. The future poet and novelist was a sixteen-year-old boy in 1856 when he joined a crowd of 3-4000 at Dorchester to watch the execution of Martha Brown for the murder of her husband.

Though no-one knew it at the time, it was to be the last public hanging of a woman in Dorset. The event inevitably made a big impression on the young Hardy, who often referred to it in later life. He was not proud of having been there, admitting in a letter to Lady Hester Pinney in 1926: 'I am ashamed to say I saw her hanged, my only excuse being that I was but a youth, and had to be in the town at the time for other reasons.' Despite the passing of seventy years, he also recalled 'what a fine figure she showed against the sky as she hung in the misty rain, and how the tight black silk gown set off her shape as she wheeled half-round and back'. The experience undoubtedly influenced Hardy's writings, especially concerning the fate of Tess, who, in his novel, is hanged for murdering Alec d'Urberville, the lover who has ruined her life.

John Brown was Martha's second husband and was twenty years her junior. She was born Elizabeth Martha Clark in about 1811, probably at Thorncombe. Her first husband, John Bearn, was twenty years her senior. They lived at Powerstock but it was a marriage blighted by tragedy. Their infant sons, William and Thomas, both died in 1835, as did James, Bernard's son from his first marriage. The fate of Bernard's daughter, Elizabeth, born in 1822, is unknown. Bernard himself died in the early 1840s and Martha subsequently worked as a housekeeper for John Symes, of Blackmanston Farm in the Purbeck parish of Steeple, where she met John Brown. He was in his early twenties, she about forty or forty-one when they married at Wareham in

January 1852. They settled in the hamlet of Birdsmoorgate, near Broadwindsor, where Martha kept a little grocery shop while her youthful husband used his horse and cart to earn a living as a carrier. Martha also suspected that Brown was having an affair with fellow Birdsmoorgate shopkeeper Mary Davies.

Brown made his last journey on 5 July 1856, when he and fellow carrier George Fooks delivered two cart-loads of poles to Beaminster. On the return journey they stopped at a pub in Broadwindsor, not leaving until 11pm and reaching Birdsmoorgate at midnight. What happened after that was disputed. Martha said she found her husband on the doorstep at 2am with a serious head wound. He muttered something about 'the horse', which she took to mean that he had been kicked by the animal, which was notoriously vicious. She claimed that she helped him into the house, where he clung on to her dress so tightly that she was unable to summon help until 5am, when she woke Brown's cousin Richard Damon, who lived 150 yards away. Brown was already dead when Richard arrived.

Damon was the first of many to visit the cottage that morning. While Martha's story was not immediately disbelieved, there were some things that didn't add up. Although Brown had bled profusely from the 'many great wounds' on his head, there was no evidence of a blood trail from the doorstep into the house or indeed from the stable where he kept the horse. There was also evidence that he had sunk to his knees and vomited after stabling the horse; his hat was also found nearby. Despite a thorough search, a blunt hatchet that Brown was known to have owned was missing.

The doubts and suspicions were echoed the following day, first in the *Western Flying Post* newspaper, then at the inquest in the Rose and Crown pub at Birdsmoorgate, where witnesses added that there was evidence of blood and brain stuck to the walls in the room where Brown was found. The inquest jury's verdict was wilful murder by person or persons unknown. Despite protesting that she was 'as innocent as the angels in heaven', Martha Brown was soon on her way to Dorchester Jail.

Reports of her trial at a packed Dorset Midsummer Assizes in Dorchester on 21 July describe Martha as a woman of 'dark complexion with scanty black curls'. She showed no emotion as she was

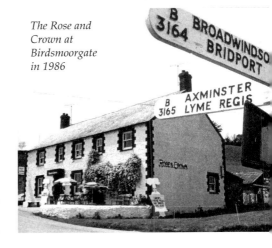

The Rose and Crown at Birdsmoorgate in 1986

led into the dock and pleaded not guilty in a 'low voice'. Although the prosecution acknowledged that the evidence against Martha was circumstantial, there was a lot of it. The existing doubts about her version were compounded by the evidence of two surgeons, who described head injuries that would have killed Brown instantly. It would have been impossible for him to struggle home from the stable, they said.

Defence counsel Mr Edwards opted not to call Martha to give evidence, no doubt fearing that cross-examination would wreck any lingering hopes of an acquittal. He called only one witness – John Symes, from Steeple, who had no direct knowledge of the case but had employed Martha as a servant for ten years. He said she was 'as kind and inoffensive a woman as ever lived' and he had been sorry to lose her.

After a four-hour retirement, the jury found her guilty of murder and the judge donned the dreaded black cap to sentence her to death. Martha again appeared unmoved and continued to protest her innocence – although as she left the dock, she admitted to a clergyman that she had made up the story about the horse. Her husband had in fact fallen down the stairs.

Between 21 July and 9 August, the date set for Martha's execution, petitions calling for a reprieve were signed in many Dorset towns and sent to the Home Secretary, Sir George Gray, but without success. Then, just two days before her life was due to end, and after several previous attempts to

John Brown's gravestone

persuade her to confess, Martha finally dictated a statement to the prison governor which, for the first time, told what was probably the true story behind the tragic events of 5-6 July.

'My husband,' she said, 'came home on Sunday morning, the 6th of July, at 2 o'clock in liquor and was sick. He had no hat on. I asked him what he had done with his hat. He abused me, and said: "What is that to you? Damn you!" He then asked me for some cold tea. I said I had none, but would make him some warm. His answer was: "Drink it yourself and be damned!" I then said: "What makes you so cross? Have you been to Mary Davies's?" He then kicked out the bottom of the chair on which I had been sitting and we continued quarrelling until 3 o'clock, when he struck me a severe blow on the side of the head, which confused me so much that I was obliged to sit down. He then said (supper being on the table at the time): "Cut it yourself and be damned!" and reached down from the mantelpiece a heavy hand-whip with a plaited head and struck me across the shoulders with it three times, and every time I screamed out and said: "If you strike me again, I will cry murder." He replied: "If you do, I will knock your brains through the window," and said he hoped to find me dead in the morning then kicked me on the left side, which caused me much pain. He immediately stooped down to unlace his boots, and being much enraged, and in an ungovernable passion at being so abused and struck, I seized a hatchet that was lying close to where I sat, and which I had been making use of to break the coal for keeping up the fire to keep his supper warm, and struck him several violent blows on the head – I could not say how many – and he fell at the first blow on his side, with his face to the fireplace and he never spoke or moved afterwards. As soon as I had done it I would have given the world not to have done it. I had never struck him before after all this ill treatment but when he hit me so hard at this time I was almost out of my senses, and hardly knew what I was doing.'

Armed with this confession, the prison chaplain hurried to London hoping to see the Home Secretary, only to find that he was away in London and that the Under-secretary, Mr Waddington, had neither the means to contact him urgently nor the power to grant a reprieve. Had she confessed earlier, and revealed the provocation that had driven her to murder, Martha may well have been spared the gallows. But the truth had come too late.

On the day of execution, Mary Davies set off from Birdsmoorgate intending to walked the 25 miles to witness the last minutes in the life of the woman who had killed her lover. She got not further than Broadwindsor, however, before being turned back by a threatening crowd – an indication of where public sympathy lay.

For her last breakfast, Martha had only a cup of tea. She declined to take the prison van to the scaffold, preferring to walk. She once again maintained her composure, talking to an emotional Rev. Henry Moule, Vicar of Fordington St George, and showing no emotion as she climbed the thirty steps to the scaffold. 'At the proper signal the bolt was withdrawn, and the unhappy woman was launched into eternity,' reported the *Dorset County Chronicle*.

Among those present in the crowd was not only the teenaged Thomas Hardy but a Mr Mills of Martinstown, who suffered from a scrofulous neck disease known as the King's Evil. In 1938 his son, a Dorchester saddler, told a local newspaper that the hanged woman's hand had been rubbed against his father's neck, in accordance with belief and custom, and had 'effected a complete cure'.

Mr Mills and Thomas Hardy are not the only ones to have been profoundly affected by Martha Brown's story. Many, even in our own time, have unexpectedly sensed her influence, including myself. While writing the Martha Brown chapter of my book *Dorset Murders* in 1986, I felt an overwhelming sense of bewilderment and rural ignorance as if I was somehow tuning into Martha's thoughts in the last weeks of her life. As a journalist and author, I have written about dozens of murders but this is the only time I have had such an experience.

In the late 1990s the bestselling novelist Rosemary Ellerbeck, then living at Sturminster Newton, became fascinated with Martha after being introduced to her by Dorset-based film-maker Nick Gilbey. She admits that they and Swanage researcher Graham Chester all became 'obsessed' with the subject and their collaboration added many pieces to the story. Under her favourite pen-name Nicola Thorne, Rosemary wrote not only a novel called *My Name is Martha Brown* but a non-fiction book *In Search of Martha Brown*. Both were published in 2000. In the same year Gilbey produced a thirty-minute documentary on Martha for HTV, which included a discussion between Rosemary, Graham and myself, filmed in the very house at Steeple where Martha worked and first met John Brown.

Even today, research on Martha continues in Dorset. It's as if this unfortunate woman has unfinished business with the county of her traumatic life and awful death.

CHAPTER FOUR

The War that Destroyed a Family

They called it the war to end all wars and it's often said that no family was unaffected by the unspeakable carnage that occurred between August 1914 and November 1918. Yet few families can have suffered more severely than the Lanes of Blandford.

When the First World War broke out, Annie Lane of Whitecliff Mill Street was already a widow who had struggled for the best part of two decades to bring up her six young sons. She had no daughters. By the time of the Armistice in 1918, four of those sons had been killed in action (two of them on the same day), a fifth had a terminal illness, the sixth was wounded and Annie herself was also dead. Even by the shocking standards of the First World War, it was a family tragedy on a grand scale.

The date of 1 July 1916 was etched into the minds of a generation. It was the day that the Battle of the Somme began. It was also the worst day in history for the British army, which suffered more than 57,000 casualties, including 19,000 deaths. Among those 19,000 dead were two of Annie and the late Frederick Lane's six sons.

One, Private Albert Sydney Lane, aged twenty-three, was married to Margaret and lived at Deanland, Sixpenny Handley. He was in the 6th Battalion the Dorsetshire Regiment but attached to the 2nd Battalion the Wiltshire Regiment. Little is known about the circumstances of his death but his body was recovered and buried in the Peronne Road Cemetery at Maricourt.

Albert Lane's gravestone

Even less is known about the death of his brother, Private Frederick John Lane, who also perished on 1 July. He was twenty-eight, married and serving with the 1st Battalion the Dorsetshire Regiment. His is one of more than 73,000 names on the Thiepval Memorial to those British and French soldiers who were killed on the Somme in 1916-17 but have no known grave. A memorial card kept by the family begins:

A sudden change, at God's command he fell
He had no chance to bid his friends farewell;
The call came without warning given
And bid him haste to meet his God in heaven.

A century later, there are no known photographs of Albert or Frederick apart from two small army pictures that appeared side by side in The *Western Gazette* on 19 July 1916 under the headline 'Illustrated Roll of Honour'. The paper reported that both brothers were killed 'in the Big Push', as the operation was known. 'Both are sons of Mrs Lane, of Whitecliff Mill Street, who has three other sons in active service. Both the deceased heroes leave widows,' the report added.

The youngest of those other sons was Private Reginald Bertie Lane, who was with the 5th Battalion the Dorsetshires. On 11 January 1917, he too died on the Somme. His body was never found and, like his brother, Fred, he is remembered on the Thiepval Memorial. In the space of six-and-a-half months, Annie Lane had seen half her family wiped out.

Her three surviving sons were also actively involved in the war, two with the Dorsets, the other with the Salvation Army. There was, of course, no end in sight to the fighting, and from the relative security of the twenty-first century, it is hard to imagine the trauma and worry which Annie must have endured. The stress must surely have taken a toll but we can only speculate that her own death 8 August 1917 might have been due to a broken heart. She was sixty-one. Her moving memorial card read:

Dear Mother, rest. Thy work is o'er,
Thy loving hands shall toil no more.
No more thy gentle eyes shall weep.
Rest, dear Mother, gently sleep.
She suffered patiently and long,
Her hope was bright, her face was strong.
The peace of Jesus filled her breast
And in His arms she sank to rest.

By a tragic irony, Annie's death contributed indirectly to the death of a fourth son. In peacetime Harry James Lane had worked for Charlie Coates, a hay and straw merchant, who had premises at Pimperne and stables on the site now occupied by Blandford Post Office. But in 1917 he was Private Harry Lane of the 1st Battalion the Dorsetshires.

When news of his mother's death reached the front, Harry was granted compassionate leave to attend her funeral. In August 1917 he returned to Blandford, where his young wife, May, was waiting for him at their home at 6 Brown's Yard, East Street. On 8 May 1918, nine months to the day after the death of her mother-in-law, May Lane gave birth to her first child, Eric. By this time, however, the baby's father was fighting for his life in a military hospital in France. Like so many of their generations, child and father were never to meet.

'I believe my father was on his way back up the line after attending his mother's funeral when he was shot in the back of the head by a sniper,' Eric (known throughout his life as Joe) Lane told me when I interviewed him for the *Blackmore Vale Magazine* in 2004. 'I think he died a long time after he was injured.'

Bill (left) and Harry Lane with Harry's wife May

Joe and Marion Lane visit Harry's war grave in France

Inset: *May Lane in old age*

In fact, Harry survived for a year in the hospital, where he amused himself by doing needlework. He finally lost his battle for life on 31 August 1918, aged thirtyy-three, and was buried in the Villers-Bretonneux Military Cemetery. His needlework was subsequently returned to his wife but has since been lost.

Harry's death left only two Lane brothers alive. Ernest, the eldest of the six, made his own contribution to the war effort as a member of the Salvation Army, carrying out catering and other duties for the troops. His eventual fate is unclear but his niece Eileen Dennis believed it was a disease or illness contracted at the front that killed him.

Eileen's own father, William Charles (Bill) Lane, was the only one of the six brothers to live to an old age, although even he did not escape the battlefields unscathed. 'He didn't talk about it much but he too was in the Dorsetshires and was badly wounded,' said Eileen. 'His eye was hanging out and he came home with shrapnel in his shoulder which gradually worked its way down his arm. He used to joke that when it came out, another war would start. It came out in 1939!'

Bill Lane became a foreman in Hall and Woodhouse's wine and spirits department at Blandford and died in 1981, aged ninety.

His nephew, Joe (full name Eric Harry Joseph Lane), meanwhile, was brought up by his widowed mother. 'It was a hell of a struggle,' he said. 'When I was at school, she went out to work and did several jobs.'

One of her employers was Brown and Drew, the bakers, and a perk of the job was the right to take home stale bread after work. She also worked in several houses as a charwoman or cleaner. May eventually remarried when Joe was a teenager and from that point on his father was rarely spoken of. May died in 1973 aged eighty-one.

Joe himself worked as under-butler at Bryanston School before the Second World War, when he joined the Royal Artillery, serving mostly in India and Burma. After the war he worked in the engineer's department of Blandford and North Dorset councils. He was in his mid-seventies when he and his wife, Marion, finally took the opportunity to visit his father's grave in Villers-Bretonneux Military Cemetery.

Even at that time, however, Joe was not consciously aware that his birth was directly linked to his grandmother's death. Until I did the sums after interviewing him at his home in Larksmead, Blandford, in 2004, and pointed out that he was born nine months after his father's return to Blandford for the funeral in August 1917, he had not worked out that he must have been conceived during this last visit home. He was deeply moved by this belated revelation.

Joe Lane died in Blandford Hospital in May 2007, aged eighty-eight. Marion died in 2013.

CHAPTER FIVE
The Boscombe Whale

As a beach attraction, Bournemouth has seen nothing like it, before or since, and few events in the seaside town's 200-year history have generated more amazement or amusement than the Boscombe Whale. But when the 40-ton leviathan was washed up on Boscombe beach on 7 January 1897, no-one could have imagined the bizarre sequence of events that was to follow. The *Bournemouth Guardian* reported simply: 'On Tuesday night the carcass of a whole whale, some 70ft long, was washed ashore at Pokesdown. During the next two days it drifted with the tide westwards and finally stranded close to Boscombe Pier.'

The whale, said to be 'of the North Atlantic variety', became an instant hit with locals and visitors alike. A reporter who covered the story recalled later: 'The stranded whale drew the multitude – scientific, ignorant and merely curious – from far and near. They came by train from the villages of Dorset and the New Forest, tramped down to the beach and wondered – and sniffed. That long, slaty slab of dead mammoth that lay parallel with the low water mark was surely one of the strangest visitors that Boscombe had ever had. Boys took running jumps up its slippery sides and tobogganed down them on the seats of their trousers gleefully. Earnest schoolteachers took parties of youngsters and gave lessons in natural history. Farmers from the Piddles poked the thick hide of the beast with sticks, and inland folk raised exclamations of astonishment at its length, its strength and its thickness.'

And all the time, the reporter added, a 'certain musty odour' filled the air and grew worse and worse. 'Disinfectants were freely pumped over it but what could you do with a mass of decaying fish the size of a canal boat?' When work began on removing the skeleton, 'the aroma became a smell and the smell became a foetid stink'.

As the crowds flocked in, the Crown laid claim to the carcass and instructed the Receiver of Wrecks to look for a buyer. He found a willing purchaser in Dr Spencer Simpson, who was prepared to part with £27 for this unusual prize. As subsequent events were to demonstrate, the medical man had bitten off more blubber than he could chew.

When Dr Simpson failed to remove the carcass, the Town Clerk began

The whale on Boscombe beach

legal proceedings against him for causing a nuisance. The doctor claimed he was seeking skilled knowledge of how to cut up the whale, sell the blubber worth an estimated £200 and preserve the skeleton. He was ordered to 'abate a public nuisance' within forty-eight hours and warned that he would have to pay the police himself if he wanted them to keep the crowds at bay.

Dr Simpson began to develop a fortress mentality, 'almost living on the beach' in order to defend his acquisition despite the unpleasant smell and growing concerns about public health. When the sanitary inspector arrived, tempers flared and Dr Simpson 'drew a swordstick, made a thrust and said he could run him through'. A policeman confiscated the weapon and charged the doctor with assault for which he was fined £1 with 13 shillings costs.

Dr Simpson next arranged for a Brighton company to carve up the beached monster and remove the bones for cleaning and display. Such was the stench that their workers had to tie bandana handkerchiefs over their noses as the ever-present spectators stepped further and further back. The workmen successfully removed the skeleton but left 35 tons of decomposing blubber on the beach. Dr Simpson tried to sell this for £200 but the only offer received was for 5 shillings from a local resident. He also hired a Poole boating firm to dump the flesh in the Wych Channel in Poole Harbour but this too ended in a court case when he was sued for the balance of the hire charge. The saga was into its fourth week when council workmen made a pre-dawn swoop to clear away the rotting blubber. Their work spread a 'vile aroma all through the town'.

By this time a tidal wave of Victorian humour had been unleashed at Dr Simpson's expense. 'Exactly what a doctor should want with a whale – and a dead whale at that – is not very easy to see,' observed a writer in The *Pick Me-Up*. 'The only explanation of his purchase I can offer is that, like so many of his profession, he is interested in the tight lacing question and wants a job lot of cheap whale bone for a new hygienic corset.'

The *Daily Telegraph* commented: 'When we remember how easy it is for a doctor not to acquire the ownership of the stranded carcass of a whale, our sympathy with Dr Spencer Simpson, of Bournemouth, in the position he at present finds himself, undergoes a sudden chill. A doctor of medicine would no doubt be more strongly tempted than a doctor of divinity or of music to undertake this responsibility; but still it is a temptation which even a medical man should have no serious difficulty in resisting. What with police expenses, fees for consulting experts, wages of labour, hire of lighters and other charges, it looks as if this piece of private property would cost its owner a pretty penny. And he will hardly find an equivalent value in the discovery – interesting as it is from the zoological point of view – that a whale is a white elephant.'

The *Daily Mail*, referring to the first court case against Dr Simpson, wrote: 'The bench, naturally jealous at having no whale of its own, sternly bade him abate the whale within 48 hours. Now a whale takes some abating. The moral of which is that a whale is a white elephant.'

Dr Spencer Simpson

The removal of the bones and blubber from Boscombe beach were by no means the end of the saga. In the summer of 1898 the bones finally returned from Brighton to be erected on Boscombe Pier, where they became a unique and popular attraction for several years before ending their days in a Springbourne scrapyard. In 1900, three years after the whale was washed ashore, the irrepressible Dr Simpson made a fresh attempt to exploit his investment by hiring the Grand Theatre at Boscombe for a concert and lantern lecture entitled *Wonders of the Deep*. Admission was 6d (2.5p) for adults and 3d for children and the audience was promised a 'great treat' – although the programme carried a warning that the concert could be subject to 'considerable alteration and curtailment'. This proved to be a whale of an understatement. The event was an unmitigated disaster and for the second time in three years the mad medic of Boscombe became a laughing stock. 'The whole affair was more than amusing, more than burlesque – it was pitiable,' commented the *Bournemouth Guardian*. 'It was a pity it was ever arranged.'

The newspaper decided to print the programme in full so its readers might understand 'how poorly the after-proceedings tallied with the promise'. First on the programme was a nine-part concert by a choir and musical society, featuring such appropriate items as *Whaler's Song*. But in opening the proceedings, Dr Simpson announced: 'There will be no choir. I don't know why.'

The *Bournemouth Guardian* commented: 'Someone ought to know, for a perusal of the programme points to a carefully planned series of selections. The postscript hardly prepared the audience for a total absence of that side of the entertainment.'

The concert over before it had begun, Dr Simpson moved swiftly to the second half of the programme, which promised such topics as whale-hunting, strandings and the habitats, habits, diets and anatomy of whales. The *Guardian* noted: 'A man well up in his subject, with some experience in lecturing and a couple of dozen good slides, could have made it very interesting.' What followed, however, was an utter shambles as Dr Simpson 'fumbled about' on the stage, made 'disconnected observations' and 'continually trotted about in front of the screen'. 'It was difficult for the adults present to keep tally with the doctor's vagaries and his numerous side remarks, or to see how, why, when or where some of them fitted into the subject matter,' said the *Guardian*.

At the start of the lecture, the curtain went up to reveal not only Dr Simpson but an admiral, an alderman and two or three men in blue Coastguard jackets plus one in white. 'Their duties were not explained,' said the *Guardian*. 'It may be that the man in white was to have been a representation of a whaler but they were not called on and during the performance somehow disappeared.' At one point the Mayor arrived but, 'evidently grasping the state of affairs', declined to take his seat and hurried off to another engagement.

The hundreds of schoolchildren present 'in expectation of an entertainment of an instructive nature' reacted with a mixture of amusement and bemusement as the show descended to the level of farce. They laughed heartily when Dr Simpson began his lecture on *Wonders of the Deep* by placing a stuffed monkey on a table and telling them it would keep an eye on proceedings. Despite asking people to tell him if he was not speaking loudly enough, Dr Simpson's lecture was 'read intermittently by the light cast from the screen and in a low tone'.

After an hour, some members of the audience were growing impatient, not least Mr W. Jones, head of the Boscombe British Schools. 'Seeing that the children had been an hour without being able to hear scarcely anything of the lecture, and considering it was rather hard, if not unkind, to keep the children there for another hour, I intimated to the lecturer that I would withdraw my scholars as quietly as possible,' he said. He began to shepherd his pupils from the gallery, only to be confronted by Dr Simpson, who had interrupted his ramblings to intervene. 'My 150 scholars were well on their way out when the lecturer appeared on the stairs and ordered the children back,' Mr Jones added. 'The result was considerable confusion and some risk of accidents.'

The story of Dr Simpson and his whale became part of local folklore and gave rise to a rhyme, which was recited by children for years to come:

Have you been to Boscombe?
Have you seen the whale?
Have you smelt his fishy smell
And sat upon his tail?

CHAPTER SIX
Hutchins' Unsung Heroine

Dorset's most famous book is the magnificent *History and Antiquities of the County of Dorset*, first published in two large volumes in 1774, revised twice and reprinted at least three times since. The first edition was the life's work of a Rector of Holy Trinity, Wareham, the Rev. John Hutchins. But how many of Hutchins' generations of readers have known that this monumental work would never have come to fruition without the heroic efforts of the author's wife, Anne? How many have been aware that the greatest work ever published on the history of Dorset owes its survival to the single-minded bravery of a parson's wife more than 200 years ago?

When the Great Fire of Wareham broke out on 25 July 1762, John Hutchins was half-a-county away, performing clerical duties in the parish of Swyre. It was one of the hottest days of the year and back in Wareham many other inhabitants were attending a service at the chapel. For many, their Sunday-best clothes would be all they possessed by the end of the day.

The fire started about 3pm when a careless servant threw hot embers onto a rubbish heap in the grounds of the Bull's Head Inn in South Street. Within minutes, fragments of burning straw had spread to a nearby fuel-house. From there the flames were carried onto the roof of the Bull's Head, setting light to the thatch.

The alarm was quickly raised but a spell of hot weather had rendered Wareham's many other thatched roofs tinder dry. Fanned by a breeze from the south-east, the fire quickly engulfed other buildings, their timber frames and plaster adding fuel. The wooden shambles and stalls in the Market Place helped take the fire into West Street and North Street. The inhabitants did their best to halt the fire, dragging burning thatch from the rooftops and dousing the flames with buckets of water carried from wells and the river. But it was not until the wind changed direction four hours later that the spread was halted.

By this time 133 houses had been destroyed and hundreds of people were homeless. Damage was estimated at the then considerable sum of £10,000. Driving over from Poole early the following day, Sir Peter Thompson wrote: 'There I saw the most dismal sight my eyes ever beheld, the greater part of the town destroyed by the fire!' Sir Peter had to leave his carriage and horses in the road and pick his way through the smouldering debris that was blocking their path. 'It was too much for my spirit,' he added. He did not stay long, turning for home without seeing any of his Wareham friends.

Among the 133 houses destroyed in the fire was John and Anne Hutchins' home, The Parsonage in Pound Lane. In her husband's absence, Anne risked her life to save her husband's notes and manuscripts, repeatedly wading into the fire to grab bundles of his precious papers. These included transcripts of records relating to Dorset, the originals of which were housed in the Tower of London. Not all of Hutchins' collection was saved but Anne rescued enough to enable her husband to continue with his county history, which he had already been working on for forty years. After learning of the fire, many people came to his aid, including some who had previously failed to respond to his requests for information. Others made cash donations to assist his research.

Hutchins pressed on with the task, despite pain and partial paralysis in later years following a stroke. Finally, in 1773, he felt able to pen the dedication signifying that his tome was finished. It was dated 1 June 1773. Sadly, he did not live to see the product of his labours in print, dying just three weeks after writing the dedication. He was buried at St Mary's church, Wareham. His *History* was published the following year in two folio-sized volumes.

Anne Hutchins survived her husband by twenty years, by which time work on a second edition of four volumes, edited by Richard Gough, was already well underway. Complete sets of this edition are extremely rare due, ironically, to a fire at the printer's in Fleet Street, London, in 1808, which destroyed all but 112 copies of the first two volumes. Most of the surviving copies have since been carved up by booksellers to extract the many fine prints for separate sale.

Far more common is the third edition, edited by William Shipp between between 1861 and 1873 and also published in four hefty volumes. A Dorset historian of our own time, Rodney Legg, described Shipp as displaying 'some impatience with the original author' and 'augmenting his work almost out of all recognition'. A four-volume facsimile of the Shipp edition – all 3000 pages of it – was published in 1973, providing access to the work to the wider Dorset public, most of whom had never set eyes on the earlier editions.

Between them, Hutchins and his continuators created one of the finest and most substantial histories of any British county. 'Subsequent historians remain in Hutchins' debt,' added Legg.

CHAPTER SEVEN
Churchill's Bridge Too Far

It was a small jump for one man but could have been a giant backward leap for mankind – an event that threatened to change the course of world history. On a rustic bridge near the Poole-Bournemouth borough boundary at Christmas 1892, a teenager called Winston Churchill made a miscalculation that almost claimed his life forty-seven years before the outbreak of the Second World War. The future Sir Winston was eighteen at the time and was staying at the Branksome Dene beach house of his uncle and aunt, Lord and Lady Wimborne. He was twenty minutes into a game of chase with his twelve-year-old brother, Jack, and their cousin, Ivor, aged fourteen, when he made the fateful decision to cross the 50-yard-long rustic bridge that spanned Branksome Dene Chine. What happened next is described by Churchill himself in his autobiography.

'Arrived at its [the bridge's] centre, I saw to my consternation that the pursuers had divided their forces,' he wrote. 'One stood at each end of the bridge. Capture seemed certain. But in a flash there came across me a great project.'

The bridge at Branksome Dene Chine

His typically audacious plan was to climb over the balustrade, grab one of the spindly young fir trees that grew up from the chine 29 feet below and slide down its trunk to the ground. 'My young pursuers stood wonderstruck at either end of the bridge. To plunge or not to plunge, that was the question! In a second I had plunged, throwing out my arms to embrace the summit of the fir tree. The argument was correct; the data were absolutely wrong. It was three days before I regained consciousness and more than three months before I crawled from my bed.'

Churchill's mother rushed down from the house, his father hurried back from Dublin and the nation's best surgeons were sent for to deal with injuries that included a ruptured kidney. 'It is to the surgeon's art and to my own pronounced will-to-live that the reader is indebted for this story,' Churchill adds.

The accident and the period of convalescence that followed are credited with having a maturing and mind-broadening effect on the young Winston. Not only did he have time to think, he was also exposed to many colleagues of his politician father, Lord Randolph Churchill. 'During this year [1883] I met at my father's house many of the leading figures of the Parliamentary conflict, and was often at luncheon or dinner when across his table not only colleagues, but opponents, amicably interchanged opinions on the burning topics of the hour,' he writes. 'It was then that I first met Mr Balfour, Mr Chamberlain, Mr Edward Carson, and also Lord Rosebery, Mr Asquith, Mr John Morley and other fascinating ministerial figures. It seemed a very great world in which these men lived…'

During the later decades of the twentieth century, the exact location of the bridge where Winston came to grief was the subject of a long-running debate among local historians, the two candidates being Alum Chine in Bournemouth and Branksome Dene Chine, a few yards inside the Borough of Poole. Most published sources give Alum Chine the verdict and Bournemouth Borough Council once considered putting a plaque and floodlights there to commemorate the incident. However, the evidence of contemporary Ordnance Survey maps weighs convincingly in favour of Branksome Dene Chine, which – unlike its rival – was part of Lord and Lady Wimborne's Canford Estate. The evidence includes maps of 1891 and 1904, which indicate that the only footbridge in that era spanned Branksome Dene Chine and that there was no bridge at Alum Chine. Further evidence comes from a 1910 history of Bournemouth, which refers to a 'rustic bridge made of timber and iron rods', which had at some point been thrown across the Branksome Dene ravine by the owner of neighbouring Branksome Tower, C. W. Packe. By 1910, however, this bridge and an adjoining embankment had 'long since disappeared'. And by the time Churchill revealed his mishap some years later, this bridge was long forgotten and local writers assumed it was the one at Alum Chine, there being no obvious alternative. Once committed to print, such myths are copied from one publication to another and are difficult to shift.

Churchill's main connection with the area came through his aunt, Cornelia (née Churchill). She married Ivor Guest, of Canford Manor, who became the first Lord Wimborne. Lady Wimborne is said to have worshipped Winston's father, Lord Randolph, who has been described as her 'favourite brother'. Winston himself was a regular visitor to the Canford Magna and Branksome Dene houses from an early age and was allowed to wander at will across the 10,000-acre estate, which stretched from the south bank of the River Stour at Wimborne to the sea. His favourite pastimes included damming streams and bricklaying, both of which he continued into adult life. His famous interest in bricklaying is traditionally associated with his country house at Chartwell but it had its beginnings at Canford, where estate workers would invite him to repair a wall or even knock down a wall so that he could rebuild it.

Once, after his Boer War exploits became well-known, Winston gave half-a-crown to a son of the Canford head gamekeeper, Mr Wren, to drive ducks so he could shoot them. Mr Wren's wife objected.

'Do you know who I am?' asked Winston.

'Pity the Boers didn't keep you,' Mrs Wren replied.

The gamekeeper feared he would be sacked and that evening went to Lord Wimborne to apologise. Lord Wimborne laughed, telling Mr Wren that at dinner Winston had told him that Mrs Wren had called him a damn fool, which was more than anyone else at the table dared to do.

Both the Churchills and their Canford relatives were heavily involved in politics, and when Winston made his maiden speech in the House of Commons in 1901, Lady Wimborne was there to support him. In the years that followed, he continued to visit Canford, often dining in the most elevated company. In 1909 he opened the Branksome Liberal Club at Poole and the same year was the main speaker at the Canford Liberal rally, when Mrs Pankhurst and her suffragettes staged a demonstration.

There are few more significant figures in Poole's history than the first Lord and Lady Wimborne. They also rubbed shoulders with the highest in the land, including royalty and leading churchmen and politicians, many of whom were entertained at Canford Manor or their luxurious town house in London, Wimborne House. As a Blenheim Churchill, Cornelia had an impressive family pedigree, but her husband's family, the Guests, derived their fortune from the South Wales iron industry. Ancestor John Guest became a furnace manager in 1767 and by 1850 his descendants controlled the greatest iron works in the world. Josiah Guest bought Canford Manor in 1846 for £335,000 and engaged Sir Charles Barry, architect of the Houses of Parliament, to rebuild and enlarge the house. The first Lord Wimborne died in 1914 and his wife in 1927, four years after she sold Canford Manor, which then became the public school that it remains today.

CHAPTER EIGHT
The Coffin in the Crypt

According to official records, the Honourable John Damer took his own life in a London tavern at 3am on 15 August 1776. The thirty-two-year-old eldest son and heir of Lord Milton, squire of Milton Abbas in Dorset, apparently shot himself in the right side of the head after dining in the company of four women and a blind fiddler in an upstairs room at the Bedford Arms in Covent Garden. He left a widow, Anne, aged twenty-seven, although the couple had been separated for some time. Their loveless marriage had produced no children.

The parish register confirms that Damer's funeral took place at Milton Abbas six days later, on 21 August. Amid much wailing and funereal pomp, his remains were laid to rest in the family vaults beneath the north transept of Milton Abbey church. But were they? Later generations of villagers disputed the official version. They not only claimed that young Damer had survived his own funeral but that he was often seen around the family home in later years. There is also reason to think that the coffin that today sits beneath the memorial to Lord and Lady Milton may contain something other than John Damer's earthly remains.

The Damer family were very wealthy. As the eldest son, John Damer was heir to an estate worth the princely sum of £30,000 a year but he seemed bent on squandering it even before he inherited. His wife's biographer describes him as 'one of a wild, foolish set about London, whose whole glory in life was centred in the curl of a coat-collar and the brim of a hat. These young fops made up for a want of wit by the most extravagant display of ridiculous eccentricity.' Damer's favourite pastimes were horse racing and gambling. Three times a day he appeared in a brand new suit and his wardrobe was sold for £15,000 following his apparent death. He ran up debts estimated at more than £70,000. By 1776, his creditors were closing in while his father – whose other two sons were also extravagant – had run out of patience and refused to bail him out.

The inquest was held at the Bedford Arms at 6pm on 15 August, fifteen hours after Damer's death in the same building, where he had been a customer for many years. There were three witnesses – the tavern keeper, John Robinson, the fiddler, Richard Burnet, and Damer's house steward,

John Armitage. Coroner Thomas Prickard and the twenty-two-man jury heard that after dining in an upstairs room after 11pm, but eating very little, Damer was entertained by the four ladies, who sang, and Burnet on the violin. The ladies left at 3am after which the fiddle player was asked to leave the room and return in fifteen minutes. Twenty minutes later, the sightless musician reported that Damer had not spoken to him following his return and that there was a 'disagreeable smell' in the room that he thought might be from a candle that had fallen over. When Robinson joined him, however, he found Damer dead in a chair, bleeding from a head wound with blood on his clothes and the floor and a discharged pistol between his feet.

Burnet reported that Damer had not been as cheerful as usual while Robinson said the note he had received the previous evening requesting the meal and entertainment had been written in a 'confused manner' and 'not like his usual manner of writing'. Armitage reported that Damer had 'for some time past appeared to be uneasy and disturbed in his mind and that his spirits were oppressed' though he could 'not account for it'. The jury returned a verdict that Damer had killed himself while 'not being of sound mind, memory or understanding but lunatic and distracted'.

Despite the verdict, there were some notable omissions from the evidence. Although some people must have been aware of his financial predicament, his probable motive for his suicide was barely hinted at. The coroner's record also makes it clear that no-one heard the pistol go off, which is surprising. But it does not tell us that 'the ball had not gone through his head', as is made clear in a letter written by Horace Walpole just five days later. There also appears to have been no mention during the inquest of a scrap of paper which, according to Walpole, was found on a table nearby and bore the words, 'The people of the house are not to blame for what has happened, which was my own act.'

The inquest was clearly less thorough than it might have been but that was not unusual in the eighteenth century and does not constitute evidence that Damer somehow faked his death to escape his debts. If there was some kind of conspiracy involved, he would presumably have needed at least one accomplice and possibly more. It was normal in those days for a jury as well as the coroner to view the body and examine any injuries before delivering their verdict and the inquest documents and other contemporary accounts suggest that this was no exception. Since it is inconceivable that the coroner and all twenty-two jurors were involved in a conspiracy, we must assume that there was a genuine corpse for them to view and that it had a head wound. However, assuming that neither the coroner nor any of the jurors knew Damer when he was alive, and since the fiddler was blind, it appears the only people present who were in a position to identify the body were

John Robinson and John Armitage. Both had known Damer for many years and had served him regularly in their respective roles. It is not inconceivable that they co-operated in some elaborate scheme thought up by Damer to fake his death – a scheme that would presumably have involved the acquisition of a body other than his own. In eighteenth century London, this would not have been as difficult as it sounds, especially if the body was 'borrowed' to be returned later.

This theory is purely speculative and may sound far-fetched. It certainly does not amount to a prima facie case in support of the claim that Damer survived and most investigators would probably dismiss the suggestion as no more than village tittle-tattle. There is, however, one piece of evidence that ensures that the Damer file cannot yet be closed.

In about 1873, a Fordingbridge gentleman called Frederick Fane was staying at Milton Abbey when he heard the legend of John Damer and the 'bogus funeral' that had allegedly taken place a century earlier. 'A more than the usual display was made at the funeral, even exceeding the displays common at the time,' he said in a talk to the Dorset Natural History and Antiquarian Field Club some years later. 'He was buried in the vaults of Lord Milton, below the north transept of the Abbey Church… However, the country people were not without suspicions, would not and did not believe that young Damer was really dead and buried, and it was believed that on many occasions subsequently he was seen in the flesh about his paternal home. At any rate, his apparent death and burial appear to have satisfied his anxious creditors that nothing farther was to be expected from him in liquidation of his debts. The people of Milton said nothing but thought a good deal, no doubt.'

At the time of Fane's stay, some repairs to the north transept were being carried out and the clerk of the works invited the visitor to accompany him into the vaults, which were usually inaccessible. Among the numerous coffins on either side of a central passage was one bearing John Damer's name and recording his death at a young age 'somewhere about 1770'. The clerk of works invited Fane to lift the coffin from the trestles on which it stood.

'This I found impossible owing to its extraordinary weight,' the visitor recalled.

'Now sir, try to lift this one,' said the clerk, pointing to another coffin nearby.

The second coffin came up 'without the slightest exertion'.

'There, sir,' said the clerk. 'This one contains a body gone to dust. The other one is full of stones, as it was supposed by the old villagers would be the case if any opportunity ever again occurred for investigation.'

As soon as the building work was completed, the vaults at Milton Abbey were sealed again and the coffin and its contents left to sit undisturbed on their trestles indefinitely. Perhaps one day circumstances will conspire to make possible the opening of the vaults once again and even of the coffin. Unless and until they do, the truth behind the legend of John Damer's death will remain a mystery.

CHAPTER NINE
The Shapwick Express

For almost a century his sporting achievements were all but forgotten but today Dorset-born Charles Bennett's role in Olympic history is recognised once again. Bennett, a train driver in his early life and later a pub landlord, became known as 'the Shapwick Express' after becoming the very first British winner of an Olympic gold medal for track and field athletics. In fact he returned from the second modern Olympiad in Paris in 1900 with no fewer than two gold medals, one silver medal and two world records.

Charles Bennett was born in the village of Shapwick, between Blandford and Wimborne, in 1870, the son of carter Henry Bennett and his wife, Peggy. The 1881 census shows that by then the family were living at Manor Farm House, West Woodyates, between Blandford and Salisbury. As a young man Charles worked as a train driver based at Bournemouth Central Station. His running career appears to have started in earnest in 1892, when he joined Portsmouth Harriers. But there are also tales suggesting that much of his early training involved chasing horses across ploughed fields, while a member of the Joyce family, of White Mill, Sturminster Marshall, described seeing 'the boy Bennett running as if his life depended on it'. Charles was also reputed to live on a diet of boiled rice with a pinch of salt plus three raw eggs and sauce.

Bennett joined Finchley Harriers, one of Britain's top athletics clubs, in 1896 and the following year won his first Amateur Athletic Association (AAA) title over 4 miles. He successfully defended the title in 1898 and 1899 and also became AAA ten-mile champion in 1899 and national cross-country champion in 1899 and 1900. Also in 1900, he won the AAA one-mile championship and qualified for the Olympic Games. His winning time of four minutes 28.2 seconds was not exceptional even then but, as one

Charles Bennett in action c1900

37

sportswriter remarked, 1900 was 'not a vintage year for milers'.

In Paris later that same year, the favourite for the Olympic 1500 metres was American John Cregan, who had produced the fastest run of the year over one mile – four minutes 24.4 seconds. But the race was on Sunday 15 July and Cregan withdrew on sabbatical grounds leaving Bennett and local hero Henri Deloge – the world record holder over 1000 metres – as the main contenders.

Bennett was well-known for hanging back in races, then surging past his rivals with a sprint finish. In Paris, however, he adopted a different tactic, leading from the front with the Frenchman tracking him all the way. Bennett's rural background had prepared him well for a course that involved three 500-metre laps of an undulating field. It was a close race but Bennett took the victory in four minutes 06.2 seconds, four-tenths-of-a-second ahead of Deloge. Officially the time was a world record, although many athletes had covered 1500 metres faster in non-metric mile races. It was also the first Olympic track and field gold medal won by a British athlete. Bennett reputedly celebrated with a visit to the Folies Bergères, the famous cabaret music hall in Paris.

Charles Bennett with some of his trophies

He won his second gold medal in the 5000 metres team race in which the British team also broke the world record. This was also on a Sunday and again the Americans withdrew on religious grounds, leaving the combined British-Australian team with only the French to beat. Bennett's silver medal came in the steeplechase in which he was in the middle of a British clean sweep of the medals. *The Guinness Book of British Olympians* describes Bennett as a 'much under-rated athlete', whose Paris double was probably the finest by a British athlete since Fred Elborough broke two world records – for 220 yards and 880 yards – in one afternoon in 1876.

Bennett's Olympic season closed with a challenge match in Manchester against Britain's 800m

Olympic gold medallist Alfred Tysoe. They met over three-quarters-of-a-mile to decide who was the nation's leading middle-distance runner. Again it was a close race which Tysoe won in three minutes 13.0 seconds. But Bennett's British record of three minutes 10.6 seconds survived. When I met him in 1994, Charles's son, Reg, then aged eighty-seven, told me his father was carried shoulder-high through the streets of Wimborne after one of his triumphs – possibly his Olympic victories.

After ending his railway career, Charles went on to run the Dolphin pub (now Gulliver's Tavern) at Kinson, Bournemouth, where his five children were born. Licensing records show he was landlord from 1903-18. He died at Kinson on 18 December1948, aged seventy-eight, and is buried in nearby St Andrew's churchyard. His wife, Sarah, died in 1950 aged seventy-five.

Bennett never boasted about his athletic achievements, which remained largely forgotten until Wimborne Athletic Club member James Eldred did some research in the early 1990s. The centenary of his Paris triumph was marked in 2000 by the Charles Bennett Millennium Mile, an elite race held in the streets of his native Shapwick at the time of the Sydney Olympic Games. Guests included 1930s' Olympians Sydney Wooderson, a former mile world record holder, and Crew Stoneley, a silver medallist at the 1932 Los Angeles Games. Both were living in Dorset in 2000. There was also a boys' race, fittingly won by Bennett's great-great-grandson, Samuel Ward.

Four years later, soon after the Athens Games, Shapwick villagers and Charles' grandson Chris Bennett officially opened the Charles Bennett Village Green. Another major running event consisting of a series of mile races was held in 2012 to coincide with the London Olympics. Three generations of the Bennett family were present and this time Charles' twelve-year-old great-great-great niece, Macy Godden, put the Bennett genes to good effect to win one of the medals. In 2014 a plaque commemorating Charles Bennett's athletic achievements was unveiled on the wall of Shapwick's village pub, the Anchor Inn.

CHAPTER TEN
The Lecherous Squire of Woodlands

An extraordinary character from Dorset's past is Henry Hastings, the rough-and-ready village squire of Woodlands, near Verwood, 400 years ago. His womanising was as legendary as his sporting lifestyle but neither seems to have done him much harm, as he lived to a ripe old age. According to the *Dictionary of National Biography*, he was born in 1551 and died at the age of ninety-nine in 1650. His neighbour, Anthony Ashley-Cooper, the first Earl of Shaftesbury, claimed he was 100. Other sources give his birth year as 1561, which would have made him eighty-nine at the time of his death. Whichever is true, he outlived the vast majority of his contemporaries.

Henry, second son of George Hastings, the fourth Earl of Huntingdon, became Lord of the Manor of Woodlands through his marriage to the heiress Dorothy Willoughby. Lord Shaftesbury, who lived at nearby Wimborne St Giles, described him as 'low, very strong and very active, of a reddish flaxen hair'. He continued: 'His clothes were always green cloth and never worth, when new, £5. His house was perfectly of the old fashion, in the midst of a large park well stocked with deer; and near the house rabbits for his kitchen; many fishponds; great store of wood and timber.'

The scope of Henry's sporting activities was limitless. 'He kept all manner of sport hounds, that ran buck, fox, hare, otter and badger, and hawks long- and short-winged,' wrote Lord Shaftesbury. 'He had all sorts of nets for fish. He had a walk in the New Forest and the manor of Christchurch; this last supplied him with red deer, sea and river fish.'

According to Shaftesbury, Hastings spent virtually all his time hunting, shooting, hawking and

Henry Hastings, the lecherous squire of Woodlands

fishing, except the time that he 'borrowed to caress his neighbours' wives and daughters'. He favoured younger women of the 'lower classes', preferably under the age of forty. Apparently there was no young woman in the area of the status of a yeoman farmer's wife or under 'but it was her own fault if he was not intimately acquainted with her'. Part of Henry's strategy was to butter up the women's menfolk. He always spoke kindly to their husbands, brothers and fathers, inviting them to his house and offering them 'beef, pudding and small beer in great plenty'.

Hastings may have been a great seducer and country sportsman but his housekeeping standards left a little to be desired. 'The great hall was strewed with marrow-bones, full of hawks' perches, hounds, spaniels and terriers,' Lord Shaftesbury said. 'The upper side of the hall hung with fox-skins of this and the last year's killings; here and there a pole-cat intermixed; guns and keepers' and hunters' poles in great abundance.'

More dogs could be found in the parlour, where most of the great chairs were usually occupied by litters of cats, who were not to be disturbed. Some of the cats always attended their master at dinner and he kept a 'little white stick that he might defend such meat that he had no mind to part with to them'.

The windows in the large parlour were littered with Hastings' bows, arrows and other equipment, while the corners of the room were 'full of the best-chosen hunting or hawking poles'. At one end of the parlour was Henry's oyster table, which was well used, as he ate Poole oysters twice a day throughout the year. At the other end were two tables and a desk on which sat a *Bible* and *The Book of Martyrs*. On the tables were hawks' hoods, bells and other paraphernalia and two or three old hats with the crowns pushed in to hold ten or twelve pheasant eggs. Nearby was a drinks closet stocked with wine and beer, although the booze was strictly rationed, as Hastings never permitted excessive drinking by himself or his guests.

Lord Shaftesbury added: 'He was well natured, but soon angry, calling his servants bastards and cuckoldy knaves, in one of which he often spoke truth, and sometimes in both. He lived to be 100 and never lost his eyesight but always wrote and read without spectacles and got on horseback without help. Until past four score, he rode to the death of a stag as well as any.'

Henry's long-suffering first wife, Dorothy, second daughter and co-heiress of Sir Francis Willoughby, the builder of Wollaton, Nottinghamshire, died in 1638, twelve years before her husband. Within six months of her death, Hastings settled part of his estate on Anne Langton, of Woodlands, the unmarried daughter of William Langton. They subsequently married but when Henry died, he was buried alongside Dorothy at the old Horton church. Their son, Sir George Hastings, joined them there after his death in 1657. There is no mention of Anne in the epitaph.

CHAPTER ELEVEN
The Reformed Highwayman

If Henry Hastings has a rival for the title of the most colourful character in Dorset's past, it is surely John Clavell, a man of many talents, who used them in an extraordinary variety of ways. He packed a great deal into his forty-two years and is probably best known for his career as a burglar, horse thief and highwayman. But although his 'ill-led life', as he called it, earned him a death sentence, he was later reprieved and turned over a new leaf to make his way as a poet, dramatist, doctor and lawyer.

Clavell – born at Glanvilles Wootton, near Sherborne, in 1601 – has long been known as a 'gentleman highwayman'. He is mentioned in passing by the eighteenth-century Dorset historian John Hutchins and by the authors of many books on highwaymen. But until relatively recent times, knowledge of him remained hazy. Most of what we know about him today is down to John Pafford, former Librarian at the University of London, who lived at Bridport from his retirement in 1971 until his death at Dorchester in 1996 aged ninety-six. Fragments of information gathered over a sixty-year period enabled Dr Pafford to piece together Clavell's story.

For John Pafford, the picture began to emerge in 1932, when a seventeenth-century manuscript arrived at the British Museum for identification. 'It was a play called *The Sodder'd Citizen*, which had long been known by name but which no-one had seen,' said Dr Pafford told me in 1993 following publication of his book on Clavell's life and works. 'I was asked to edit it and was able to show that it was pretty certainly the work of John Clavell.'

The five-act play, based on Clavell's life as a highwayman reformed, was published in 1936 and gradually other material began to come to light. Whenever any information came his way, Dr

John Clavell aged twenty-five

Roundchimneys, John Clavell's home at Glanville's Wootton

Pafford made a note of it. Over the years, he developed a 'certain admiration' for his subject. 'He was constantly active and he pulled himself together and made good,' he said. 'I have a lot of respect for him, although he was boastful and cocky and in some ways never grew up.'

Clavell, the fourth of five children and the only surviving boy, was born into a good family described by Hutchins as boasting an 'antiquity not to be equalled in this county and very rarely in any other'. He was the nephew and heir apparent of Sir William Clavell, owner of Smedmore House near Kimmeridge in the Isle of Purbeck, who seems to have shared some of John's energy and eccentricities. Sir William was a scholar and poet and a gentleman soldier knighted for his part in dealing with an Irish rebellion. He was also a less-than-successful entrepreneur whose various schemes – the extraction of alum from Kimmeridge cliffs, the production of salt by boiling sea water and the use of Kimmeridge shale to fuel a glassworks – brought him to the brink of ruin.

John Clavell's home was the Manor House at Glanville's Wootton, later called Golden Grove and now known as Roundchimneys. It stands a mile north-east of the parish church. His early home life was not as stable as it might have been. There were financial problems and a document dated 1617 states that his father, also John, 'hath for many years past lived from his wife and with a woman whom he keepeth in his house, for which he hath been publicly reproved by the Justices of Assizes'. Such was the seriousness of this offence that John Clavell Snr had been 'driven out of Dorset for the cause aforesaid' and was now living in Somerset. Dr Pafford believed John Jnr's later misdemeanours stemmed from his broken home and his 'unsatisfactory father'.

The report that documents John Snr's dubious lifestyle also implies that Sir William's was not dissimilar. He too was living apart from his wife and not setting the example expected of a man in his elevated social position. He was nevertheless outraged when, in later years, he learned of his nephew's crimes.

At eighteen, young John Clavell became a student at Brasenose College, Oxford, but while there was convicted of breaking into the treasure house and stealing the college plate. According to his own account, he later fell victim to moneylenders and financial tricksters, running up debts and eventually finding himself in the debtors' prison at Newgate. There is also an account of him running penniless through the streets of London, pursued by the representatives of a moneylender.

His other recorded crimes include a robbery at Aylesbury, Buckinghamshire, in 1624, when he was accused with a labourer, Thomas Morris alias Price, and was himself described as 'late of Beaconsfield, gentleman'. A year later he robbed Thomas Tench of £92 on the highway at Edgware in London. He was also charged with stealing horses at Westminster.

One source alleges that Clavell led a gang responsible for a series of 'frequent and insolent' robberies in the London area in 1625. 'This record shows little of the glamour of the romantic highwayman; but although that glamour was no doubt always largely fictitious, the daring thief, then as now, made some appeal to the popular mind,' wrote Dr Pafford.

In later life Clavell himself wrote that highwaymen were popularly known as 'knights of the road', held in awe by the public and known to inn servants as 'captains'. It's clear that he wished to be remembered as a gentleman-highwayman.

By February 1625 Clavell had been declared a felon and forced to forfeit his estate. The following year he was sentenced to death at the Court of King's Bench but was fortunate enough to lodge a plea for mercy at the time of a general amnesty linked to the coronation celebrations of King Charles I. He languished in jail for two years but was then pardoned and began the reformed phase of his life.

Clavell was already married to a girl of humble origin called Joyce, who had not only helped him to obtain his reprieve but nursed him through sickness. Joyce meant everything to him and he wrote about her at length as he pursued his career as a writer. Evidence from Clavell's notebook – including payments for doctors, nurses and a midwife and a bill for funeral expenses – suggests that she may have died in childbirth in 1634. This would also explain a moving elegy to a lady he has lost, penned by Clavell at about that time.

He later moved to Ireland and married a Dublin heiress, Isabel Markham, who was only nine years old. Her father, a wealthy vintner, was a friend of the Lord Chancellor, which led to Clavell being made a barrister in November 1635. He conducted a number of legal cases in London and Dublin, where he represented his uncle in property lawsuits.

Clavell also practised as a physician and his writings include twenty-three pages of prescriptions and other medical matters, some claiming to have cured various people. He also wrote prose and verse and *The Sodder'd Citizen*, a five-act play clearly based on his own life as a highwayman reformed, and publicly performed by the King's Company in 1630.

His talents were recognised at the highest level and he became something of a celebrity. One of his works, *A Recantation of an Ill-led Life; or a Discourse of the Highway Law, in Verse*, was 'approved by the King's most excellent majesty and published by his express command'. It was written while Clavell was still in prison – 'from my lonely chamber in the King's Road, October 1627' – and includes a personal appeal to the King for mercy. It appears to have been a success in every respect, probably helping to secure his release, perhaps by impressing the King himself, and running to three editions following its publication in 1628.

John Clavell died in 1643 of pleurisy. It is not known where he is buried.

CHAPTER TWELVE
The Durweston Poltergeist

They prompted national headlines at the time and 120 years later, the spooky events that unfolded in the village of Durweston, near Blandford, over the course of several weeks in 1894-5 remain among the most dramatic, intriguing and convincing poltergeist episodes on record. The disturbances began in relatively modest fashion on 13 December 1894, when a widow called Mrs Best noticed the faint sounds of knocking and scratching in various parts of her semi-detached cottage. Over the next few days the strange noises were repeated several times, gradually increasing in volume until even the gamekeeper next door, Mr Newman, heard them along with the village blacksmith, who said the sounds were 'as heavy as sledgehammer blows'.

Mrs Best, aged about sixty, was a kindly Christian woman, who lived with her grown-up daughter at Norton, just outside the main village of Durweston. The pair of white-walled cottages still overlooks the Stour valley

The white cottage at Norton overlooking Durweston, where the poltergeist activity began in 1894, is also a local landmark

and is a familiar landmark, visible for miles around. In 1894 Mrs Best agreed to become foster mum to two orphaned sisters, Annie Cleave, aged twelve or thirteen, and her sister, Gertie, who was four. A third sister, Lizzie, who was two years older than Annie, had already died of consumption or tuberculosis, the great killer of the Victorian age. Annie herself was not in the best of health, a doctor describing her as being 'of a markedly consumptive tendency' and 'hysterical'.

As December wore on, events at Norton became ever more bizarre. Mrs Best was startled when a number of stones flew through the windows, breaking the glass before returning of their own volition through the round holes they had made. Neighbours searched the area in case there was a prankster at large but could not find even a footprint. On 18 December, Annie reported seeing a boot come out of the garden plot and strike the back door, leaving a muddy mark. During a visit to Mrs Best's house, neighbour Mr Newman saw a 'big blue bead' strike the window but not break it. He then sat down and told the poltergeist: 'You're a coward, you're a coward; why don't you throw money?' Newman then saw a 'quantity of little shells' come through an open door from the garden, arriving at intervals of 30 seconds to a minute and travelling at about 5 feet above the ground. 'They came very slowly and when they hit me I could hardly feel them,' he told an investigator from the Psychical Research Society. 'With the shells came two thimbles. They came so slowly that in the ordinary way they would have dropped long before they reached me. They came from a point, some, I think a trifle higher, and some no higher, than my head. Both the thimbles struck my hat. Some [of the shells] missed my head and went just past and fell down slantingwise, not as if suddenly dropped. Those that struck me fell straight down.'

Next a slate-pencil, about two-and-half inches long, came from behind Mr Newman and landed in a bowl on the pantry floor. Then a hasp – 'like the hasp of a glove' – dropped into the gamekeeper's lap from somewhere above his head. Finally the woman's boot, which had lain outside the door since the earlier incident witnessed by Annie, began moving a foot above the ground towards Mr Newman and landed gently beside him. Mrs Best threw the footwear – described as 'an old, dirty boot from off the garden plot' – outside. The gamekeeper followed, putting his foot on it and defiantly announcing: 'I defy anything to move this boot.'

'Just as I stepped off, it rose up behind me and knocked my hat off; there was no-one behind me,' said the incredulous gamekeeper. 'The boot and the hat fell down together.'

A few days later Mrs Best and her foster children moved into Mr Newman's cottage, where they were twice visited by the Rector of

Durweston, the Rev. W. M. Anderson, who was hoping to witness the phenomena. On his first visit on 4 January, nothing happened but when he returned with the village schoolmaster, Mr Sheppard, on 10 January, the poltergeist wasted little time in making itself known.

Following the two men's arrival, Mrs Best put the two girls to bed and lay alongside them with her head at the opposite end. When loud rappings were heard on the walls in different parts of the room, Mr Sheppard went outside to make sure no-one was playing tricks while Mr Anderson remained in the bedroom, where he was able to feel a vibration while holding the rail at the foot of the bed. The vibration varied according to the loudness of the knocking. The Rector searched both cottages thoroughly, reporting only an occasional noise as if someone was scratching the wall with their nails. 'This scratching also appeared to be produced on the mattress of the bed, although I am sure it was not produced by any of the three occupants of the bed, as I could see their hands and watched them very closely all the time,' he said.

Mr Anderson observed that to start with the rappings frequently stopped when he came into the room but after a short time his presence made no difference. The sounds went on, 'loud and continuous', for much of the night. At 2.15am, Mr Sheppard imaginatively suggested asking the 'agency' if it would write any communication on a slate. It was invited to deliver a specified number of raps for a 'yes' and, remarkably, did so. This was a poltergeist with intelligence. It was also patient enough to wait for a slate and pencil to be brought from Mrs Best's house and bright enough to respond to a series of questions as to where the slate should be placed. 'Every conceivable place in the room was suggested one after the other,' said the Rector, 'but the right number of raps was not given, but a short, sharp knock, which seemed always to be given for a negative. We almost gave up at this point until, as an afterthought, I suggested the window-sill, which was at once accepted.'

Responding to another series of questions, the poltergeist indicated that only Mrs Best and the two girls were to remain in the room and the light was to be removed. The others made their way downstairs but the bedroom door was left open. Within fifteen seconds, and in almost pitch darkness and 'amid perfect silence', the investigators heard the sound of pencil scratching on slate. Mrs Best uttered a 'suppressed groan'. The signal indicating that the writing had finished was four sharp raps, and at the very moment that these were delivered, the sound of the pencil dropping on the slate was also heard, followed immediately by the screaming call of 'Come!' from Mrs Best.

'I was in the room instantly, the whole thing taking less time than it would take to read this description,' said Mr Anderson. 'The light showed some unmeaning scratches on the slate. We asked for something legible, which was promised in the usual way.'

Mrs Best reluctantly agreed to repeat the exercise on condition that the Rector stayed on the stairs. This time the presence produced a 'flourish' on the slate: curves that were 'beautifully drawn' with firm, bold lines such as no child could produce'. When the exercise was repeated a third and a fourth time, the words 'MONY' and then 'GARDEN' appeared on the slate. Neither Mrs Best nor Gertie could read or write; Annie was literate but Mr Anderson was convinced that no-one had moved in the bed, which was 4 or 5 feet from the window-sill, let alone left it. Mrs Best offered to take a solemn oath confirming this in case anyone doubted it. There being no further rapping, the witnesses left the gamekeeper's cottage at 2.50am. A subsequent search of the garden yielded no money.

On Christmas Day 1894, Annie and Gertie went to stay with the Cross family in the main part of the village. For a while nothing untoward happened but in early January, after the girls had been back to Norton for one night and returned to the Cross house, scratching sounds were heard in their room and then plaster fell from the walls and ceiling onto their heads. They were moved to a different room only for the scratching to resume the next night, despite the presence in the room of Fred Cross, an adult son of the host family, and a light. The travelling poltergeist then went quiet again until 15 January.

That evening, with the girls in bed upstairs, Fred and his mother and sister heard several taps in quick succession. 'I at once went to the children, finding them all asleep, although a loud knock after I got into the room awoke the eldest orphan,' he recalled later. 'The knocks being repeated, we sent for a few friends to come and hear the noises. The eldest orphan, while dressing, awoke the little one. I gave her several questions to ask the agency (as it would not reply to anyone else), a large number of which were answered by an agreed number of knocks. There was no-one except the small child (who was still in bed) within a distance of at least 5 feet from the spot where the knocks came from, except when it hit the door against which I was standing. A light was burning all the time and Mr Sheppard, our schoolmaster, was in the room when the last of the questions was answered.'

The rappings continued 'at intervals' until just after midnight, the last knock coinciding with the arrival of the Rector. There were no noises the following night but on 17 January, events took an even more extraordinary turn with the poltergeist demonstrating a musical talent. 'As soon as I was in bed, the knocking began again, keeping time with any tune which was well-known by the children,' said Cross. 'I asked for several comic, school and sacred songs, which were all answered by raps on the head of the bedstead for each single note. The only tune we asked for which was not rapped out was *The British Grenadiers*.'

Throughout this bizarre episode, a light was burning in the room and Fred was holding the children's hands to make sure they weren't doing the knocking. The knocking ceased soon after midnight but began again next morning, when requested songs were again rapped out.

Gertie Cleave was taken away that afternoon, Annie the following Monday. It is probable that the sisters never met again. Annie initially went to stay with a woman at Iwerne Minster, where the disturbances resumed. These included noises on the outside walls of the house, a large stone thrown at the porch roof and snowdrops dug from the garden and thrown about. On 7 March 1895, an inspector of boarded-out children took Annie to stay at her flat in London. Official records suggest that 'no disturbance worth recording' took place there but a later source claims that the girl displayed 'highly developed powers as a medium'. All sources agree that she died soon afterwards of consumption. What happened to Gertie is unknown.

Poltergeist is a German word literally meaning 'noisy or rattling spirit'. There are numerous cases on record, including the widely witnessed Winton Poltergeist in Abbot Road, Bournemouth, in 1981. The phenomenon is often referred to by parapsychologists as 'recurrent and spontaneous psychokinesis'. Poltergeist incidents usually involve the spontaneous movement of objects and are generally associated with an individual, unlike ghosts and hauntings, which are more typically linked to a property or location and tend to manifest in a different (and less spectacular) way. In many cases that individual is a child, often a child who is disturbed and/or in puberty or adolescence. Given her age, background and health, and a doctor's description of her as 'hysterical', Annie Cleave appears to have ticked more than one of these boxes. Alcoholism, drug addiction and intense sexual energy can also be triggers. It is as if surplus or suppressed energy is being harnessed and redirected by some unseen force.

While ghosts can hang around a location for years, poltergeist activity rarely continues for more than a few weeks, and that is again the case here. Such activity can also be witnessed by anyone present whereas ghosts are usually perceived only by those who are sensitive to such things.

The Durweston Poltergeist's ability to communicate directly is not unique. Sir William Barrett, who investigated a series of disturbances at Derrygonnelly, Ireland, in 1877, reported that the 'energy or entity' always responded to him with the correct number of raps even though 'I mentally asked it, no word being spoken'.

CHAPTER THIRTEEN
The Runaway Rector

There is nothing like a naughty vicar story to set tongues wagging, and the gossips of Blandford and district must have had jaw fatigue in 1912. For eighteen years, the Rev. W. M. Anderson had been handing out spiritual wisdom to his parishioners in Durweston and Bryanston – including advice on the importance of their marriage vows. So it came as a shock to the rural community when the married clergyman eloped with his lover – and robbed his curate and parishioners into the bargain.

We know about the elopement through the diaries of Julietta Forrester, wife of James Forrester, Lord Portman's agent for the Bryanston Estate. For decades Julietta secretly documented everyday life in Victorian, Edwardian and post-Edwardian Dorset in her diaries, which remain largely unpublished.

The elopement is first mentioned in the entry for 25 January 1912. Betraying the incredulity that she shared with her fellow villagers, Julietta wrote: 'Received a letter from Mrs Oborne saying that Rev. W. Anderson had gone off on Wednesday with Mrs Axford, Lord Portman's coachman's wife. There had been talk about them for some time. He said he had loved her for seventeen years! It seemed incredible! Lord and Lady Portman were in London that day at the wedding of one of Lady P's sons. I never thought of Mrs A behaving so but Anderson was bad enough for anything! I believed he had sold his soul to Satan over the Durweston Ghost!'

This was a reference to the Durweston poltergeist, described in the previous chapter. The Rev. Anderson was among those who had taken the events seriously, unlike the sceptical Mrs Forrester.

Mrs Axford, who ran off with the Rector of Durweston and Bryanston

On 3 February 1912, Julietta noted that Lord Portman was 'very disgusted' with Anderson 'after all he had done for him, paying for him to go abroad etc. About two years ago, on hearing of the intimacy between Anderson and Mrs Axford, Lord P spoke to the former about it but A denied all the charge. Mr Heber Percy also spoke to him with the same result.'

The more charitable of his parishioners might have forgiven Anderson for his inability to resist the lure of love but less forgivable was the theft of his curate's pay packet and some of the money from the Coal Club fund to finance the elopement. He had also 'left his wife, his mother and his sister destitute', according to Julietta.

Her diary continues: 'Axford [the coachman] had spoken to Lord P about a divorce but as he had actually seen his wife off by train when she left him (because people should not say they had parted bad friends or that he had driven her from home!), Lord P told him he had connived at the elopement and therefore would be unable to obtain a divorce. The two [Anderson and Mrs Axford] had first gone to Halifax to her brother's but he refused to take them in and where they went then did not appear to be known.'

According to the late Pete Sherry, a grandson of coachman James Axford and his wife, the hostility to the runaway couple was such that a crowd threatened to tar and feather them as they waited on the platform at Blandford station. Speaking to me in 2012, two years before his death, Pete,

Lord Portman's coachman James Axford

of Maperton, near Wincanton, confirmed Julietta's claim that they were turned away at Halifax and added that they then spent the next six months staying at the Pump House in Bath. At one point, according to the diarist, Mrs Axford made a brief return to Bryanston hoping to collect the younger of her two daughters, Constance. The child refused to leave. 'I suspect Auntie Con hung on to my mother and said she wouldn't go,' Pete told me.

It appears that in the short-term Anderson continued to draw his pay. 'By all accounts,' Julietta wrote on 17 February, 'he will remain Rector and draw his stipend as long as he is let alone – and the "unfrocking" is a costly affair and has to go through the Court of Arches.'

From Bath, Anderson and his lover sailed to Canada and ended up in Montreal, where the former clergyman eked out a living as an artist. He died just seven years later and Mrs Axford took a job as lady-in-waiting to the Molson family, owners of North America's oldest brewing company. She eventually returned to the UK with a substantial pension from Molsons of £7 10s a week. She bought a house at Malvern Link in Worcestershire, where she was secretary of the Bridge Club until she died aged ninety-eight. She spent the war years in Bath.

James Axford, a diminutive man who stood just 4ft 10in or 4ft 11in tall, retired in 1923 with a pension from the Portmans of £1 a week for life. He subsequently lived with his elder daughter, Winifred, and her family at West Orchard, near Shaftesbury, and later at Maperton, where he died in 1936 and was buried in the churchyard in an elm coffin made by his own hand.

Pete Sherry recalled: 'I remember him ever so well. He was a terrific horseman and he taught me to ride ponies. He would never talk about my grandmother. He was very strict about that and even paid a solicitor to make sure she never got in touch with the family. We used to get dollars from "Auntie in Canada" but I guessed she was my grandmother.' After James Axford's death, his estranged wife was accepted back into the family, being introduced not as Winifred's mother but as 'Auntie'.

The Rev. Anderson, meanwhile, had failed to impress Julietta Forrester from the start. On 15 October 1893, soon after his arrival as parish priest, she wrote: 'In the afternoon we went to Bryanston Church where our new Rector Mr Anderson put in his first appearance. I liked his appearance and voice. I wish I had liked his sermon.'

Julietta also implies that Anderson neglected the Bryanston half of his patch. After he and his wife took a month's holiday in Scotland in 1895, she commented: 'I thought he might have found a change in visiting his flock at Bryanston.'

When the parishes teamed up to play Blandford at cricket in 1895, 'our Rector, Mr Anderson, declined to play because he was afraid of the weather!'

St Nicholas' Church, Durweston

The result suggests the team could have done with his sporting services. After Blandford declared their innings at 300 for 9, the Durweston and Bryanston XI were skittled out for 70 runs.

After a committee meeting at Durweston Rectory to discuss the recent tea and sports in 1897, Julietta wrote: 'At the close Mr Anderson very sanctimoniously referred to the success of the entertainment and the pleasant way in which all had passed off. I think he fancied that I had meant to be disagreeable – at any rate I could tell by his nasty manner that something was intended. Mrs Anderson contributed her fling at me by saying how especially good the bread and butter and cake were at the tea. I had had nothing to do with either but I was responsible for the tarts.'

A few weeks after the elopement in 1912, Julietta wrote, a little cryptically: 'I told the Portmans about Anderson levering out so many innocent people from the parish on the charge of immorality and they roared over the story of Miss Godwin [the church organist] sticking the photo of the Rector over the head of Our Lord, which the photographer had sent on the mounts to some photos of Durweston Church, which Miss Godwin was selling for the CMS [Church Missionary Society] funds.'

The list of former rectors in Durweston church shows the Rev. W. M. Anderson holding office from 1893 to 1911, when he was succeeded by B. F. S. W. Pinney.

CHAPTER FOURTEEN

The Waterway That Never Was

When canalmania swept the country towards the end of the eighteenth century, few corners of England remained untouched. The rapid progress of the Industrial Revolution fuelled a spectacular growth in trade and that in turn required better transport links as raw materials and new products were moved around the country. Canals proved a swifter, more efficient alternative to horse-drawn wagons lumbering along poorly maintained roads or tracks. In the course of eighty years, 4000 miles of canals were constructed, becoming the arteries of commerce for an increasingly industrialised nation. They helped to transform not only the national economy but local economies all along their routes. More than two centuries later, the network is enjoying a new lease of life through the popularity of canal holidays and as havens for wildlife.

We can only imagine how Dorset would have been transformed had the canal boom reached the county – and it very nearly did. The feasibility of the proposed Dorset and Somerset Inland Navigation was first discussed at a meeting at the Bear Inn, Wincanton, Somerset, in January 1793. The original plan was to provide a waterway link between the ports of Poole and Bristol – an alternative route to the long and hazardous sea voyage around the Cornish coast. Supporters of the scheme believed they could depend on a regular traffic in coal from the Bristol and Somerset coalfields to Dorset and potter's clay from the Purbeck area needed in the Potteries district of Staffordshire. Other regular cargoes envisaged included freestone and lime from Somerset and timber, slate and wool from Dorset.

Initially there was great interest from potential investors with subscriptions greatly exceeding the prescribed minimum. Those present at the meeting were declared eligible to become shareholders, as were the owners of land involved in the proposal and residents of parishes along the chosen route.

A first route put forward ran from Bath to Frome (with a branch to the Mendip collieries) and on via Wincanton and Henstridge in Somerset and Stalbridge, Sturminster Newton, Lydlinch, King's Stag Bridge, Mappowder, Ansty, Puddletown and Wareham to Poole Harbour in Dorset.

Wareham's citizens voted to support the route but at Blandford Forum people had other ideas. Blandford held its own meeting at the Crown Inn and insisted that the canal would be more beneficial to both its proprietors and the county if it went from Sturminster Newton to Poole via Blandford and Wimborne instead of to Wareham.

Robert Whitworth, the project's consulting engineer until he resigned in September 1793, also favoured the Blandford option. His costing for the 37 miles from Freshford to Stalbridge was £100,234. The remaining 33 miles from Stalbridge to Poole had an estimated cost of £83,353. The Blandford route was finally decided upon in 1795 but with branches to Wareham and Hamworthy.

It probably seemed like the perfect compromise. However, there was still strong opposition from some landowners in East Dorset, in particular from Lord Rivers. He offered his agreement only on condition that 'the canal did not proceed beyond some point betwixt Sturminster and Blandford, otherwise withholding his consent'. As a result, a drastic decision was taken in 1796 to abandon the southern section of the canal, reducing its length to 48 miles and the cost to £146,018. It would now terminate at Gain's Cross, south of Shillingstone, thus defeating the original object of the project – the provision of a link between Poole and Bristol.

With £73,000 already raised from shareholders, the necessary Act of Parliament was quickly obtained and received royal assent on 24 March 1796. The act gave the Dorset and Somerset owners the right to draw water from any source within 2000 yards of their canal and to create a junction with the Kennet and Avon Canal, thus connecting it to the main network. It also authorised them to raise £150,000 in shares and to borrow an additional £75,000 using the canal and its anticipated revenue as collateral.

Work on the Mendip collieries branch began in the summer of 1796 at Cote in the parish of Stratton. A newspaper advertisement reported that progress was rapid, the public would soon begin to experience the benefits of the canal and 'part of it near the collieries is already completed and a barge was launched there on Monday'.

The advertisement proved to be optimistic in the extreme. Of the original £70,000 pledged by prospective shareholders, only £58,000 was forthcoming. Some tried unsuccessfully to recover their deposits of one guinea (£1.05) per share.

Over the next few years, mainly due to the nation's preoccupation with the war with France, the Dorset and Somerset company lurched from one financial crisis to another and managed to complete only 8 miles of their canal.

'The proprietors were bound by their Act to complete this part of the line first and they confidently anticipated their funds would have been sufficient for the purpose,' reported a pamphlet published some years later. 'But from the difficulty they experienced in collecting the subscriptions and the advance which took place in the price of wages, they eventually found it would cost £18,000 more than they possessed to complete the one branch of the projection.'

Progress was further hampered and expenses increased by the rocky and uneven nature of this part of the proposed canal. In fewer than eight miles it was necessary to build twenty-eight bridges of various types, three tunnels, an aqueduct, eleven grooved stop-gates, nine double stop-gates and three balance locks.

Construction finally ceased in 1803, when the last of the money ran out, although hopes lingered on until the mid-1820s, when attempts were made to involve the canal company in plans for a railway covering the same route. In the event even these plans foundered and it was another thirty years or so before the rail link came to fruition. By then the Dorset and Somerset Canal – originally described as 'one of the best conceived undertakings ever designed for the counties of Dorset and Somerset' – was reduced to an overgrown relic extending 8 miles into the Somerset countryside.

The canal company's records suffered an even worse fate. They were destroyed by a bomb that fell on Wincanton during the Second World War. One of the few surviving documents is an original plan for a double-arched aqueduct over the Sturminster Newton to Blandford road at Fiddleford. The canal would have been fed at this point by water from the Darknell Brook. The plan also shows a ford where a stone bridge is today and two houses that still survive.

CHAPTER FIFTEEN
The Tuckton Tolstoyans

A redundant waterworks in a suburb of Edwardian Bournemouth seems an unlikely location for a propaganda machine run by a colony of Russian exiles with plans for a bloodless revolution. The group's members were disciples of the writer and non-violent anarchist Leo Tolstoy and their aim was to bring about social transformation in their homeland. They lived communally at Tuckton House in Saxonbury Road, Tuckton, under the leadership of the exiled Vladimir Chertkov, formerly a wealthy landowner in southern Russia, an officer of the Imperial Guard and a favourite at the Russian court.

Towards the end of the nineteenth century, Chertkov gave up his aristocratic life and became a social reformer, devoted to alleviating the poverty and intellectual starvation of Russia's vast peasant population. He worked closely with Tolstoy, who is best known as the author of *War and Peace* and *Anna Karenina,* but also campaigned for peaceful anarchy, declaring that 'the State is a conspiracy designed not only to exploit but above all to corrupt its citizens' and that he would 'never again serve any government anywhere'. Tolstoy also understood the importance of 'education and the printing press'.

Chertkov (sometimes spelt Tchertkoff) first met Tolstoy in 1883 and it was a life-changing moment. He embraced the master's philosophy so wholeheartedly that he was sometimes said to have become 'more Tolstoy than Tolstoy himself'. Before long he had become Tolstoy's editor and agent and together they set up a publishing company called Intermediary, which attracted the support of many other great Russian writers, such as Chekhov, Korolenko, Garshin and Leskov. The aim was to provide better and affordable literature for the peasants and to campaign on behalf of various persecuted religious sects.

But Chertkov's activities made him a marked man. His house was invaded and he faced a future under police surveillance in the obscurity of a small Baltic town. Instead he opted for exile and in 1897, with thirty fellow intellectuals, fled to England, a country whose tradition in free speech he greatly admired. The group initially set up a collective at Purleigh, Essex, where they launched the Free Word Press, using an imported typeface to

A rare, faded picture of Russian revolutionaries at Tuckton House

publish books and pamphlets in the Russian language.

In 1900 the Tolstoyans relocated to Tuckton, a suburb of Bournemouth, where Chertkov's mother, Countess Chertkov, already had a holiday residence. The fledgling resort, with its coastal climate and acres of pine trees, also had a reputation as a destination beneficial to people suffering from consumption or tuberculosis and other chest ailments. Chertkov hoped the pines and soft, warm air would benefit his wife Anna's delicate health.

The peaceful revolutionaries set up a printworks in the Old Waterworks in Iford Lane and there launched their Free Age Press, which produced English language texts alongside the Free Word Press. The output was prodigious and included not only books and pamphlets by Tolstoy and his followers but a sixteen-page newspaper that was banned in Russia. The material was distributed to Russians all over the world and much of it was smuggled into Russia. Some copies of the newspaper were printed on thin rice paper so they could be folded into four, fitted into an envelope and sent through the post to Russia masquerading as ordinary letters.

The Tolstoyan community included university professors, doctors, journalists and students, many of them refugees or exiles. They numbered between twelve and thirty at various times and included not only Russians but Poles, Lithuanians, Estonians, Austrians, Finns, Dutch, Danes, French,

Germans and even a few English people. They also included a grandson of Leo Tolstoy himself.

At Tuckton House, members of the colony practised a relatively spartan lifestyle, sharing their possessions and shunning personal comforts. Their living rooms were plainly furnished with deal tables and chairs and they slept on basic army beds. They lived on an exclusively vegetarian diet, growing their own food and sharing their simple meals with visitors.

One Bournemouth resident who knew Chertkov described him as a 'very cultured and highly educated man' who was 'absolutely sincere in his efforts, as were his Russian friends'. Mrs V. Ray, of Ringwood, writing to the *Bournemouth Evening Echo* in 1968, remembered attending a party in 1920 hosted by a Jewish girl called Deana Levin, whose parents had lived in the colony for some years.

'There was a decided air of mystery about the place,' Mrs Ray recalled. 'They were charming people but nobody was quite clear about their circumstances. There was a vague idea that they were Russian refugees.'

Some of the Russians took an interest in local football and had links with Tuckton Football Club, whose ground adjoined the Old Waterworks. One of them – possibly Chertkov himself – caused a minor sensation at one match against the Charminster Road Congregational Club by putting a 2 shilling (10p) piece in the collecting box. That would have been an impressive sum more than 100 years ago.

Tuckton House, demolished in 1965, included a strong-room designed to provide maximum security for the colony's secret papers, among them Tolstoy's manuscripts. The room had walls of reinforced concrete 18 inches thick, a steel-grill door and no windows apart from a narrow iron-barred slit for ventilation. Alarm bells were switched on every night.

'The strong-room was fire-proof, damp-proof and even earthquake-proof,' says a newspaper report written at the time of demolition. 'Had the bowels of the earth or the heavens burst, and that house fallen, this room might have been left, toppled but intact. It cost far more than has been spent on modern buildings housing priceless documents. But such value was placed on Tolstoy's works by his friends that they sacrificed their personal wealth to preserve them.'

The strong-room was so effective that even demolition of it proved a challenge. After working in it for a week, two workmen had succeeded only in cutting a hole 15 inches in diameter.

The documents printed in Iford Lane almost certainly played their part in the run-up to the Russian Revolution in 1917, which in turn led to the rise of the Soviet Union – although the people who printed them did not condone the violence that unfolded.

Vladimir Chertkov remained at Tuckton only until 1908, by which time the Tsar had granted a pardon to Russian exiles and it was considered safe for them to return. Chertkov was reunited with Tolstoy and worked with him until the writer's death in 1910, aged eighty-two. Chertkov's work after the Russian Revolution included editing an edition of Tolstoy's complete works that ran to ninety volumes. Chertkov died in Moscow in 1936, also aged eighty-two, but his son, Vladimir Chertkov Jnr, corresponded with Southbourne resident Charles Preece until the 1960s.

While most members of the colony returned to Russia with Chertkov in 1908, a few stayed on to continue the work, most notably a young Estonian called Ludvig Perno. He managed the Free Age Press until 1917, when he travelled to Russia with high hopes for the future. As a pacifist, he must have been greatly disappointed with the atmosphere of turmoil and violence that awaited him. His views put him in fear of his life while his schoolteacher wife was imprisoned in Siberia.

In 1918 Estonia became a republic, independent of Russia, and in 1920-21 Ludvig worked in the Foreign Ministry in the capital, Tallin, and as an English interpreter. From 1922-24 he worked at the Estonian Embassy in London before he and his wife returned to Bournemouth. Their daugher, Maikki, married an Englishman and their son, David Walsh, still lives in the area. Ludvig – known to relatives in Estonia as 'Luti' – died in Bournemouth in 1970.

Meanwhile, Chertkov's mother also returned to England as an exile in 1917 following the execution of her husband by the Tsarist regime. She was herself out of favour with the authorities after devoting much of her considerable wealth to the cause of slum improvement in St Petersburg. She moved into her Tuckton summer residence, *Slavanka*, where she stayed until her death in 1922, aged ninety-one.

Tuckton House became a nursing home in 1929 and was replaced by bungalows following its demolition in 1965. The Old Waterworks became a motor vehicle body-building workshop from 1918 and was converted to three houses in 1989.

CHAPTER SIXTEEN
The Body in the Bank

Wimborne had never seen a funeral like it and has not seen the like of it since. There were two graves but only one body; the coffin-bearers were clad in overalls; there was an unseemly row between the undertaker and the Clerk to the Burial Board; and not a single mourner turned up at the town cemetery, although a large crowd of curious and mostly female spectators watched proceedings from the street 100 yards away. Such was the bizarre send-off for the man at the centre of what the *Bournemouth Daily Echo* called a 'shocking triple tragedy on a farm near Wimborne'.

Frank Hawkswood Burdett was already well-known in Wimborne before the tragic events that unfolded in October 1930. He had arrived in the town, apparently from Exeter, in the early 1920s, moving into a cottage at Dogdean, between Wimborne and Furzehill. He set up in business as a leather-worker and renamed his modest cottage Handicraft House. He used the title 'Captain' and talked vaguely of his army days, although no-one discovered the details of his service or the name of his regiment; he boasted that the Queen was among his regular customers; he held sales of work in aid of ex-servicemen but apparently pocketed the money himself. In his spare time he canvassed for the Conservative Party.

Burdett may have been well known but he was not well liked. His arrogance had alienated many townsfolk and he had even been banned from his local, the Horns Inn in Burts Hill, after telling the licensees how to run their business. The best of his few remaining friends were the Holloway

Handicraft House, home of Frank and Trixie Burdett

family – Thomas and Louisa, four of their six grown-up sons and the younger of their two daughters, Beatrix Mary, known as Trixie, all of whom lived at Walford Farm, on the edge of Wimborne near the foot of Burts Hill.

Burdett was a regular guest of the Holloways until 1929, when events took a turn that alienated even these most loyal of friends. The issue was a burgeoning romance between Burdett, who was fifty-eight in 1929, and 18-year-old Trixie. It was a development that shocked Thomas and Louisa Holloway to the core, not least because Burdett was old enough to be their daughter's grandfather. They banned Burdett from their home but, to their dismay, this served only to escalate matters. First Trixie – still a minor in 1929 – moved out of Walford Farm and into Handicraft House. Then her parents initiated court proceedings against Frank Burdett for abduction. Trixie responded by applying under the Guardianship of Infants' Act for permission to marry her lover.

The Holloways eventually pulled out of the court proceedings and reluctantly consented to the marriage, which took place at Wimborne Register Office on 28 May 1930. Thomas Holloway never again spoke to his son-in-law and Louisa only did so for Trixie's sake, lending Burdett, unbeknown to her husband, various sums of money, on one occasion as much as £18 – a significant sum in 1930.

Burdett was consistently failing to make ends meet since Trixie's arrival and was running up debts around Wimborne. After his death, his young wife revealed that he had become 'very worried' about the money problems. He was also annoyed by his in-laws' reluctance to help him. Several times, after drinking whisky, he announced to Trixie that he would 'shoot the whole lot of them'. She laughed it off, refusing to take the threat seriously.

Trixie had no cause to laugh when she woke early on Monday 20 October 1930. It was 4.45am, she had a headache and by the light of a candle she could see her husband getting dressed. Asked what he was doing, he replied that he was going for a ramble around Furzehill, as he could not sleep. Unusually, he gave her 'several fat kisses' before leaving and borrowed her torch and scarf. She looked out of the window and saw him heading for Walford Farm.

Trixie felt increasingly uneasy as she lay in bed. At 5.30 she went downstairs and tried to telephone Wimborne police station. It took fifteen minutes to get through and while she was waiting she noticed an envelope with the word 'Will' written on it. Fearing that her husband was intent on suicide, she left the cottage to search for him. Her search only ended when she met a policeman on his way to see her. The news he gave her was even worse than she had feared.

It was just before 6am when Thomas Holloway woke his sons and told them they were late for their milking duties. He was about to return to his own bedroom when he heard his wife scream. As he rushed into the room, his sons heard a second scream. The screams were 'punctuated by two loud shots'.

Alfred Holloway, aged twenty-six, leapt out of bed and ran to his parents' room. He pushed the door open about a foot and saw Burdett, shotgun in hand. 'I will have you all – one at a time,' shouted his brother-in-law.

With impressive presence of mind, Alfred held the door shut and ordered his brothers to escape. Only when all three were safely away did he release the door and rush out himself. Two of the brothers headed for the cow-stalls with Burdett in pursuit. 'As we got to the end of the shed, I saw Captain Burdett aiming at me with a gun,' twenty-two-year-old Ernest Holloway recalled later. 'I went straight through the door, jumped over the hedge and met a police officer down the road.'

Police found Thomas and Louisa, aged sixty-one and fifty-one respectively, still in their nightclothes, both dead and both with a shotgun wound to their chests. Burdett's own demise was less swift. Police found him 100 yards away in Muddy Lane, part of what is now the Allenview Road housing estate. The borrowed double-barrelled shotgun lay between his legs and the injuries it had inflicted were horrific. The whole of the left side of his face had been blown off, yet he was still conscious, groaning, trying unsuccessfully to speak and making gestures with his hand. It was three-and-a-half hours before he died at the Wimborne Workhouse Infirmary just across the River Allen.

From his pockets, police recovered several letters and four unspent shotgun cartridges, which they believed were intended for the Holloway brothers. Two days later Trixie – earlier described by the *Daily Echo* as 'prostrate with grief' – and two of her brothers gave evidence to a coroner and inquest jury, who returned a verdict of 'pre-meditated and wilful murder and suicide'.

The verdict was to have a direct bearing on Burdett's funeral later that day. It was scheduled for 2pm but it was 4 o'clock before his coffin arrived by lorry at Wimborne Cemetery, accompanied by workmen in blue overalls. A black shroud covered the coffin, which bore a single wreath and a card from Trixie with the poignant message: 'In loving memory of my darling husband, from his wife. Rest in Peace.'

Funeral director B. Elcock and his men were met at the cemetery by the burials clerk, A. G. Taylor, who ordered that the burial must not go ahead in consecrated ground owing to the suicide verdict. Mr Elcock reminded him that the burial fee had already been paid and that suicides had been buried in consecrated ground in the past. The waiting vicar was consulted and, after further debate, Elcock declared: 'Then we will bury him in unconsecrated ground.'

He despatched his men for picks and shovels and ordered a second grave to be dug beyond the edge of the cemetery. It was 5.45pm before the digging was completed, and even then the grave was only 4 feet deep. Meanwhile, news of the impending burial quickly spread around the town and curious spectators hastened to the edge of the cemetery. The majority were women but there were a few men. Some arrived with their infants in prams and pushchairs.

As darkness fell, Burdett's remains were lowered to their final resting place 4 feet underground in what is now the steep, grassy bank between the cemetery and Stone Lane. 'Earth to earth, dust to dust, ashes to ashes,' muttered undertaker Elcock in the absence of the vicar. Almost nine decades later, thousands pass within a few feet of

Trixie Burdett and three of her brothers at their parents' funeral

the unmarked grave every day without knowing of its existence or the story behind it.

On the day after Burdett's chaotic funeral, the atmosphere was contrastingly different as Thomas and Louisa Holloway were laid to rest following a service in the Minster. 'The whole of Wimborne and the countryside was in mourning,' reported the *Daily Echo*. The parish magazine recommended that 'silence is best in the presence of an overwhelming tragedy', which had 'shocked Wimborne to its depths'.

The crowds outside Wimborne Minster for the Holloway funeral

CHAPTER SEVENTEEN
The Bettiscombe Skull

The late Rodney Legg called it 'the most famous piece of Dorset folklore' and few would disagree. Yet almost 150 years after it was first made public, the origins of the Bettiscombe Skull are still shrouded in mystery. The Dorset folklore historian John Symonds Udal first wrote about it somewhat cryptically in 1872, describing a 'carefully preserved human skull' but identifying its location merely as a 'farmhouse in Dorsetshire'. He added: 'The peculiar superstition attaching to it is that if it be brought out of the house, the house itself would rock to its foundations, whilst the person by whom such an act of desecration was committed would die within the year. It is strangely suggestive of the power of this superstition that through many changes of tenancy and furniture the skull still holds its accustomed place "unmoved and unremoved".'

Udal subsequently identified the farmhouse as an old manor house at Bettiscombe, a small village in the Marshwood Vale about 6 miles from Bridport, and his original source as a woman who had often stayed in the house in her youth. He also recounted the legend of a former tenant who, in 'incredulity or anger', once threw the skull into a duckpond opposite the house. A few days later he was seen 'stealthily raking out the pond until he had fished up the skull', which he then restored to its customary place in the house. Udal wondered if the noises were caused by the bats, owls and other wildlife that roosted or nested in the attic or by some other 'agency'.

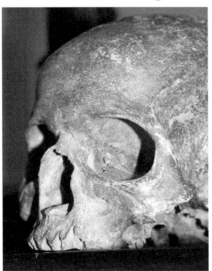

The Bettiscombe Skull

Udal, a High Court judge, gave less credence to a later story that the skull had been heard 'screaming'. It became known as the 'Screaming Skull' and 'attained other proportions so foreign to its simple origin that I almost regret ever having called attention to it'.

Writing in 1891 from Fiji, where he briefly served as Attorney-General and Admiralty Advocate before becoming Chief Justice of the Leeward Islands in the Caribbean, Udal recalled his first viewing of the skull. He had taken its reputation seriously enough to enlist the support of the local rector, who joined him on the visit together with a second clergyman. After being led up an old oak staircase, they were surprised to find the skull 'grinning at us' from the attic stairs rather than in the attic itself. They were told this was because of the 'ruinous condition of the timbers', which rendered a visit to the attic a 'journey of no inconsiderable danger'. With the owner's permission, and seemingly taking his life as well as the skull in his hands, Udal 'carefully picked my way by the aid of a lighted candle, followed by my companions, over the crazy and broken floor to where, on a niche by the side of the huge chimney-breast, lay a brick – the old shrine of the skull – upon which I reverently placed it; and there I had the satisfaction of seeing it on more than one visit in later years.'

There have been several theories concerning the skull's origins, the most popular being that it belonged to the 'faithful black servant' of an early owner of the house, a member of the Pinney family. According to this account, Pinney had lived abroad for some years and brought the skull home with him as a 'memento of his faithful follower'. Coincidentally, twelve years after his first viewing of the skull, Udal was carrying out his duties in the Leeward Islands when he stumbled across a sugar plantation on the island of Nevis known as Pinney's after its eighteenth-century owners. In a nearby church, he also found a memorial to John Pinney, born in 1686, the only son and heir of Azariah Pinney. Azariah himself is commemorated in Bettiscombe church but is best known for his part in the abortive Monmouth Rebellion in 1685. Condemned by the infamous Judge Jeffreys to be executed at Bridport, he was subsequently reprieved on payment of a £65 fine and became a slave in the West Indies. However, he wasted no time in fathering a son and turning his life around to become a successful businessman with slaves of his own. His son became Chief Justice of Nevis. The plantation remained in the family until 1800, when John Frederick Pinney sold up and retired to Bettiscombe. Understandably, Udal could not resist the temptation to join the dots. 'May not one's imagination easily lead one to believe,' he mused, 'that it was the skull of the old "Bettiscombe", the slave purchased by him in 1765, taken by his old master to the very place, indeed, from which his trusty servant had taken his name, as a memento of his humble follower?'

Bettiscombe Manor

During one of his later visits to Bettiscombe Manor, Udal and his companions made a careful examination of the skull. It was small and 'afforded no trace of the facial angle which marks the full-blooded negro'. 'Although none of us were doctors, we came across the respectful conclusion that it was *not* that of a negro,' he said. They also concluded it was a woman's skull, which tallied with another story Udal was told – that the skull had belonged to a young woman who had died or been 'made away with' after a long period of confinement in the house. He believed it was indeed a woman's skull and that a partitioned-off hiding place or 'priest's hole', measuring 15 feet by 12 feet and close to its resting place in the attic, lent a 'certain amount of corroboration' to this story.

This account is also consistent with more recent research. After studying the skull in 1963, thirty-eight years after Udal's death, a professor of human and comparative anatomy at the Royal College of Surgeons wrote: 'The skull is complete except for the mandible and a break in the left zygomatic arch. The whole bone structure is rather lightly made and the muscle markings are not prominent. It is probably a female skull aged between 25 and 30 years... I think all these quantitative data lead to just one conclusion: that this is a normal European skull, a bit small in its overall dimensions but certainly not negroid.'

In his book *Mysterious Dorset*, published in 1987, Rodney Legg put forward another theory, quoting Dr Anne Ross, lecturer in Celtic Studies at Southampton University, who had been involved in the archaeological excavation of an Iron Age temple on nearby Pilsdon Pen, the highest hill in Dorset. She said: 'It was an extremely prominent part of the Celtic religion. The severed head was particularly significant. It was believed that the Celtic gods appeared there – that it was the seat of the soul. Skulls were supposed to have magical powers when connected with fertility. They were placed in wells for this purpose.'

The present owner of Bettiscombe Manor, Lady Caroline Conran, believes the skull to be that of an Anglo Saxon woman.

CHAPTER EIGHTEEN
The Shapwick Monster

Residents of an East Dorset village still talk of the day, more than 300 years ago, when a strange creature struck terror into the hearts of their forefathers. The curious creature was discovered on Badbury Down, near Shapwick, by a workman trudging home at dusk on 12 October 1706. He quickly alerted his neighbours and soon half the village had turned out, armed with sticks, stones and other makeshift weapons.

It was Old Hobson who first spotted the fearsome beast. He reckoned it had a dozen legs or more and wisely warned his companions not to get too close. The crowd willingly kept their distance, standing 50 yards back as they peered excitedly at the intruder. None had seen the like of it before.

Farmer John suggested sending for a retired shepherd called Howe. If anyone could identify the monster, he could. The poor old chap had been bedridden for years but he reluctantly agreed to contribute the benefit of his considerable experience to the crisis. Being unable to walk, he was transported to the scene in a wheelbarrow pushed by 'a careful driver for steady wheeling most renowned'.

The barrow came within 30 yards of the creature, but then the crippled sage suddenly spluttered: 'It's a land monster, wheel me off! Wheel off, I say, or we're all dead men!'

At that very moment a stranger appeared, a travelling fishmonger, who had passed that way some time earlier. The people of Shapwick looked on in amazement as he courageously seized the sideways-walking creature and threw it in his basket.

'You fools,' he told them. 'Don't you know a common crab when you see one? 'Twas lost from my basket on the way back from the coast this morning.'

The villagers never lived down their foolishness and the story became part of local folklore. It even gave birth to a proverb as a 'Shapwick monster' came to mean an uncommon or inexplicable object. To this day there is a Crab Farm on Badbury Down. The whole hilarious tale was also recorded in verse form, at least two versions of which survive. The following version was published with illustrations in the nineteenth century:

The Land Monster
In every clime and country known,
'Tis held men most esteem their own;
A county, town, and parish, too,
Is held tenacious to their view.
But of the parish this befel,
Bespeaks them quite irascible,
To take such umbrage at a word,
That's full a century on record;
Record – I mean a word of terror
The other day, to son or father;
But to be brief, let this prevail,
I'll therefore beg to tell my tale.

Once on a time, it happened so,
Perhaps a hundred years ago,
A monger who was forced to ride,
His fish to sell, on commons wide;
Trotting along, (by fortune crossed),
One of his finest crabs he lost,
As he was riding down to Bere,
Near Shapwick town, in Dorsetshire.
Just as bright Sol was going down,
Returned from work a country clown,
Trudging along in simple nature,
Just trod upon the crawling creature;
The Crab he crawled, which made him start,
Against his bosom bounced his heart;
While panic, fear, assailed his mind,
Sideway, like crabs, some yards reclined.
The sight so strangely did appear,
He thought the devil had been there;
His hair erect, stood bolt upright,
As if he really had seen a sprite:
Then praying for some more assistance,
He stood and viewed him at a distance,
Resolved to go to Shapwick town
In haste to make the wonder known;
Which done – the people all did hie,
This hideous 'monster' to descry.
With sticks and stones, those silly elves

Collected, to defend themselves,
Just got in sight the place to see,
Where they supposed him to be;
Old Hobson, who before had found him,
Cried – 'That is he, pray don't surround him,
For he is swift of foot and sure,
He's got a dozen legs or more.'
The crab a thymey bank had found,
When crawling on the fragrant ground.
With fearful eyes they him regard,
Though at a distance 50 yards;
They unto one another swore,
They never saw the like before.
Oh then did sprake the Farmer John –
'The Shepherd Howe's the likeliest man,
He'll tell, if any in Shapwick can;'
But how to get him was their fear,
He'd kept his bed a dozen year.
They straight unto the shepherd went,
And told the sage their full intent,
Praying he would not them deny,
To go the 'monster' to descry.
The shepherd, struck with vast surprise,
Seemed first unwilling to arise;
But by recital of their prayer,
Consented to be carried there.
The carriage that they go, we find,
Was one of the wheel-barrow kind;
Such was the carriage got in haste,
For coaches then was not the taste.
A careful driver next they found,
For steady wheeling most renowned;
Then in they put the ancient sage,
Whose head was silver'd o'er by age.
So on they go, with all the town,
Encircling the poor shepherd round;
But when the Crab the shepherd viewed,
Near 30 yards from where it stood,
Unto the man did straightway cry –
Lest, fearing he should wheel too nigh –
Exclaimed in haste, and choked with cough –

'It's a land monster, WHEEL ME OFF;'
Emphatically replied again,
'WHEEL OFF, or else we're all dead men.'

Just at that time the man came back
Who lost the crab from off his pack;
He seized the Crab, with haste he snatched it,
And eager flung it in his basket.
But when the crowd perceived the man
Take up the crab, they straightway ran
In haste to hear the 'monster's' name,
And how he dared to touch the same.
'You silly fools, can it be so,
A fish so common not to know?
This is a crab, caught in the sea;
This morning it was lost by me.
So many fools upon the green,
At one time sure was never seen.'
Confused they on each other look,
And rapidly the Down forsook,
Leaving the monger far behind,
The fun to ponder in his mind.
The people, to this very day,
In Shapwick town, I'll boldly say,
Won't bear to hear the smallest hint,
Without their smelling some affront;
But what they think the greatest scoff –
Are those emphatic words – 'Wheel off.'
If any say it as they passes,
Ten to one he's mobbed by asses.

CHAPTER NINETEEN
She Who Sold Seashells

Everyone is familiar with the old tongue-twister that begins 'She sells seashells by the seashore' but few know that it reputedly has a Dorset origin. The 'she' in Terry Sullivan's 1908 verse was Mary Anning of Lyme Regis and the 'seashells' were the fossils that made her one of the most famous women in Dorset history – and one of the ten British women who have been 'most influential in the history of science', according to the Royal Society. And she achieved her success despite a background of poverty, a life punctuated by tragedies – and despite being a woman, which was a major disadvantage in most areas of life 200 years ago.

The 'Fossil Woman of Lyme' was born in May 1799 and named after her eldest sibling, also Mary, who had died in agony a few months earlier after her clothes caught fire and she was horrifically burned. She was four. The second Mary and her brother Joseph, born in 1796, were the only two of ten children born to Richard and Blandford-born Molly Anning that survived to adulthood. Joseph's descendants include Sir Crispin Tickell, a former British Ambassador to the United Nations and one of Mary's biographers

In August 1800, when she was fifteen months old, Mary was at the centre of another tragedy. A travelling equestrian show was in town and the little girl was watching it from the arms of a neighbour, Elizabeth Haskings, when the elm tree under which they were sheltering was struck by lightning. Elizabeth and two other women were killed. Other spectators rushed the infant to her home, where she was revived in a

Mary Anning, the 'fossil lady of Lyme Regis'

73

hot bath, a doctor declaring her survival miraculous. According to her family, the previously 'dull' and sickly Mary blossomed after the incident, becoming 'lively and intelligent' apparently as a direct result of the lightning strike.

Richard Anning was a cabinetmaker by trade but, like others in the Georgian holiday resort, supplemented his income by selling 'curios', as the fossils found in the area's crumbling Blue Lias cliffs were known at that time. He had a little table outside his shop in Bridge Street, as noted by the novelist Jane Austen in her diary following a visit in 1804. As Joseph and Mary grew older, they helped their father with his stall and fossil-hunting, and after his death in 1810 from tuberculosis and injuries sustained in a fall on the cliffs, they and their mother continued the little business.

Richard had left the family destitute and on poor relief, and the fossil sales provided a lifeline. In 1811 Joseph discovered a 4ft skull that he thought belonged to a crocodile. A few months after that Mary found the rest of the skeleton, which turned out to be a fine example of an ichthyosaur. The story that it was the first of its kind discovered is a popular myth but it attracted great attention and caused quite a stir at a time when some were starting to question the traditional belief that the Earth was created in six days just a few thousands ago. The Annings sold the specimen for £23, a significant sum in the early nineteenth century.

The family's income stream was less than steady, however, and after a lean year on the fossil front in 1819-20, they were on the point of selling their furniture when one of their regular customers stepped in. To ease their plight, Lieutenant Colonel James Birch from Lincolnshire sold his entire collection of fossils for £400 'for the benefit of the poor woman [Molly Anning] and her son and daughter at Lyme, who have in truth found almost all the fine things which have been submitted for scientific investigation'. The collection included the second of three ichthyosaurs found by Mary, which alone made £100. One of the ichthyosaurs has since been viewed by tens of millions of visitors to the Natural History Museum in London.

Birch's sale helped to put the Annings on a firmer footing. While her brother found work as an upholsterer, Mary continued to comb miles of cliffs and seashore in a daily search for fossils that she could sell. It was dangerous work and she once narrowly survived a cliff fall that killed her dog. As well as the three complete ichthyosaurs, her major finds also included two plesiosaurs, the first of which was the first to be discovered anywhere. It was sold to the Duke of Buckingham for £100. Five years after this, in 1828, Mary found a rare gliding reptile, the pterodactyl, and a fish called the squaloraja, which at the time was interpreted as a transition between the shark and the ray. Mary also found many ammonites, star-fish and other marine creatures. She correctly identified coprolites as fossilised faeces and discovered that belemnite fossils contained fossilised ink sacs. The leading geologist Sir Henry De La Beche used fossils found by Mary Anning as the basis for his historic 1830 watercolour of prehistoric wildlife.

Mary was known not only for her ability to locate fossils but her exceptional skill in extracting them and putting the pieces together. She was still only twenty-five when Lady Silvester wrote: 'The extraordinary thing in this young woman is that she has made herself so thoroughly acquainted with the science that the moment she finds any bones she knows to what tribe they belong. She fixes the bones on a frame with cement and then makes drawings and has them engraved.' The Lyme Regis historian George Roberts wrote of Mary's 'great judgement in extracting the animals, and infinite skill and manipulation in their development'.

From her teenage years onwards, Mary's discoveries and abilities attracted attention from the gentry and the scientific community and provided her with a bridge across the class divide. This may have gone to her head somewhat. After joining Mary on a fossil hunt in 1831, the young diarist Anna Maria Pinney wrote that this 'woman of low birth' had been 'noticed by all the cleverest men in England, who have her to stay at their houses, correspond with her on geology etc. This has completely turned her head, and she has the proudest and most unyielding spirit I have ever met with… She glories in being afraid of no-one and in saying everything she pleases. She would offend all the world, were she not considered a privileged person.'

The King of Saxony was one of many elevated visitors to what was once described as her 'little dirty shop, with hundreds of specimens piled around, and in the greatest disorder'. After writing her name in the King's physician's pocketbook, she told him: 'I am well known throughout the whole of Europe.'

Alongside this arrogance was a touch of bitterness that her knowledge was often taken advantage of and that she did not receive the recognition she deserved. Anna Maria Pinney added: 'She says the world has used her ill and she does not care for it. According to her account, these men of learning have sucked her brains, and made a great deal by publishing works, of which she furnished the contents, while she derived none of the advantages.'

As a woman, Mary was ineligible for fellowships of either the Geological Society or the Royal Society. There was some belated recognition, however. In 1835 the British Association for the Advancement of Science in Dublin raised £200 for her by private subscription. And in 1838 her friend William Buckland persuaded no less a figure than Prime Minister Lord Melbourne to donate another £300 which, combined with the earlier sum, gave her an annuity of £25. The Geological Society organised a further subscription in 1846.

By this time, sadly, Mary Anning was a sick woman. For a few years there had been talk that she had a drink problem. The truth is thought to be that she was taking ever-larger doses of laudanum to deaden the pain of the breast cancer that was finally to claim her life in 1847, aged forty-seven. She had survived her mother by just three years and was followed to the grave two years later by her brother.

A year after Mary's death, her close friend Sir Henry De La Beche, who had spent many days accompanying her on fossil hunts, used his presidential address to the Geological Society to pay tribute to her. Though 'not placed among even the easier classes of society' and having to 'earn her daily bread by her labour', he said, she had 'contributed by her talents and untiring researches in no small degree to our knowledge of the great Enalio-Suarians, and other forms of organic life entombed in the vicinity of Lyme Regis'.

CHAPTER TWENTY
Ferndown Zoo and Other Animals

Whether it was a moonlit night as the three men made their way home at Ferndown in the early 1950s is not recorded, but there was certainly enough light for two of the trio to identify the exotic beast that stood before them. The older man had blurred vision after an evening's drinking at the Angel Inn but the senses of his two sons were unimpaired. As former Ferndown businessman Alan Dean once explained to me, 'The lads were assisting their father home from the Angel when they turned into a footpath. Suddenly they saw this bear standing smack in the middle of the path. There was a ditch on either side of the path and the lads just dropped their father in the road and dived for cover – one into each ditch. They shouted, the bear went off and they raised the alarm.'

The Himalayan black bear (which was later recaptured) would have been either Rupert or Mary who, along with Ajax the lion, were Ferndown's most famous residents sixty or seventy years ago. They were among the star attractions at Ferndown Zoo, which had been opened as a 'pets' corner' by Mrs Dorothy Sadler in 1947 but had quickly got out of hand. By 1952 leopards and a gorilla were also among the larger inmates on a site adjoining Mrs Sadler's home, Sunnydale, between Ringwood

Dorothy Sadler and friends feeding Himalayan black bears Rupert and Mary.
Photo: *Bournemouth Daily Echo*

Road and Ferndown Common.

Economically, the zoo proved a great asset to the area, attracting 10,000 visitors a year, many from the established tourism destinations of adjoining Bournemouth, Poole and the New Forest. Mrs Sadler added a children's playground to the attractions and opened a shop selling teas and ice-creams. But Ferndown was in the early stages of a suburban growth spurt that was to turn it from a modestly sized village at the end of the Second World War into a town with a population of 18,000 today.

Ajax the lion. Photo: *Bournemouth Daily Echo*

While many of Ferndown's longer-standing inhabitants were happy to put up with country smells (or even jungle smells), some of the newcomers were less enthusiastic. The repeated escapes of Rupert and Mary did not help Mrs Sadler's cause, and neither did Ajax's legendary roaring which followed his weekly de-worming procedure. 'At 10am every Friday they used to give him his worming pill and starve him for twenty-four hours and he just used to roar and roar,' Alan Dean told me. 'He made such a shocking row. You had to close the windows.'

After much protest and debate, including a public inquiry in January 1955, the Ministry of Housing ordered Mrs Sadler to close her zoo. Many of the animals went to Chessington Zoo but rehoming Ajax, Rupert and Mary proved a greater challenge. By the closing weeks of 1955, hopes were fading and it looked as if the unfortunate trio would have to be put down. The solution came through an unlikely source – the BBC. On 5 December 1955, the creatures' plight was featured on an early edition of the long-running television programme *Panorama*. Mrs Sadler was inundated with offers of new homes, some rather more suitable than others. In the end all three remaining animals headed for a new home at Butlin's holiday camp in Skegness. The site of Ferndown Zoo is now occupied by the houses of Longacre Drive.

Ferndown seems to have been quite an eccentric community in those days, boasting not only a zoo but a nudist colony in West Moors Road, a mink farm and Europe's biggest duck farm on the land now flanked by Dudsbury Avenue and Glenmoor Road. The 20,000 ducks on Alan Tice's farm supplied feathers to the makers of pillows and quilts all over Europe. The area was well suited to ducks, being very boggy and dominated by rhododendrons right across to New Road.

Even before the closure of Ferndown Zoo, the community found itself with a new cause for protest and discontent. In 1954, following the closure of Tice's duck farm, Len Matcham, a Poole councillor and a director of Poole Speedway, bought some of the land and opened a mink farm there. The story goes that Mrs Matcham asked her husband for a mink coat and he replied that they could 'grow it ourselves'. He visited Stapehill, where Terry Smith farmed 10,000 mink, bought a few breeding pairs and took them to his home in the well-to-do Poole neighbourhood of Canford Cliffs. The arrival of these vicious, smelly animals prompted protests from his neighbours so Matcham decided to do the job properly and start his own farm at Ferndown. He did his research, went to the USA and returned with £35,000 worth of silver mink.

In his book *Ferndown: The Back of Beyond*, former *Wimborne and District News* reporter Brian Davis recalls: 'The Ferndown farm flourished, but it caused a bit of a stink – literally and metaphorically. Local householders complained about the smell and claimed that some of the animals were escaping. The parish council recorded objections to the farm in their minutes of September 1955, and three months later discussed further complaints concerning "an objectionable odour". Stories about the mink stink appeared in national newspapers, and in February 1956 four councillors met Mr and Mrs Matcham at the farm.'

The councillors were persuaded that the mink were kept in good conditions, that the farm's layout and maintenance were of a high standard and that the bad smell might come from other sources. But the protests kept coming and in September 1957 the owners agreed to close it and move their stock to a new site at Burley in the New Forest, where they would also have room to expand. The old site is now buried under the houses of the Dorset Park estate.

CHAPTER TWENTY-ONE

Stalbridge and the Father of Chemistry

He is one of the great names of scientific discovery, remembered by everyone who has had school chemistry lessons. Robert Boyle is best known as the man who gave his name to Boyle's Law, the revelation that the volume of a gas varies inversely to its pressure. Despite his fame, few in Dorset know that the man also known as the 'Father of Chemistry' spent much of his youth in the county and carried out his early experiments there.

Robert Boyle, born at Lismore Castle, Ireland, in 1627, was the fourteenth child and youngest son of one of the richest men in the kingdom, the self-made Richard Boyle, first Earl of Cork and Lord Treasurer of Ireland. His association with Dorset began nine years later, when his father bought Stalbridge Park and its Jacobean manor house for £5000, possibly as a refuge in case of trouble in Ireland. Lord Cork, who already owned vast estates in Ireland, also bought nearby Templecombe Manor in Somerset for £20,000 and Annery House, near Bideford, Devon, for £5000.

Stalbridge was Dorset's fifth biggest manor house but was in 'great decay' and the Earl spent a small fortune on repairs and improvements. The alterations and refinements were intended for his youngest son and the estate was conveyed by indenture to Robert Boyle two months before his fourteenth birthday.

Robert spent much of his youth in Dorset and by the age of nineteen was planning serious study on the scientific front, which needed the creation of a laboratory at Stalbridge. Letters to his sister, Catherine Lady Ranelagh, written in 1646, tell us that his plans were temporarily frustrated, first by the delayed arrival of his 'Vulcanian implements', then by the loss of his great furnace, which disintegrated during its journey to Stalbridge. 'I see I am not designed to the finding out the philosopher's stone, I have been so unlucky in my first attempts at chemistry,' he noted. Persistence paid, however, and by 1649 he was able to write to his sister: 'Vulcan has so transformed and bewitched me to make me fancy my laboratory as a kind of Elysium.'

Boyle's work was encouraged by his association with the scientific sets of London and Oxford, where he found 'a knot of such ingenious and free philosophers who do not only admit and entertain real learning but cherish and improve it'. He conducted many experiments at Stalbridge and elsewhere and wrote a vast number of published works, ranging from scientific books and papers for the Royal Society to philosophical and theological works and even a spiritual romance called *The Martyrdom of Theodora and Didymus*. Boyle's *Occasional Reflections on Several Subjects*, which deals with such diverse rural topics as horseshoes, angling and boys swimming with air bladders, was partly written during a holiday at

Robert Boyle

Stalbridge and was also the inspiration for Jonathan Swift's satirical *Occasional Meditations on a Broomstick*. 'His [Boyle's] works alone may make a library,' commented the antiquary and natural philosopher John Aubrey, one of Boyle's contemporaries.

It was a remarkable career, especially in the light of the poor health that dogged Boyle for most of his life. One contemporary described him as 'tall of stature but slender, and his countenance pale and emaciated'. For forty years he 'laboured under such a feebleness of body and lowness of strength that it was astonishing how he could read, meditate, try experiments and write as he did'. He also had a 'weakness of the eyes', spoke with a slight hesitation and had a memory 'so treacherous that he was often tempted to abandon study in despair'.

Boyle never married and left his Stalbridge estate to his eldest surviving brother, Richard, second Earl of Cork and first Earl of Burlington. He died in London in 1691 aged sixty-four and is buried in St Martin's in the Fields.

Stalbridge House, sadly, was demolished in 1822 but the park is still guarded by two stone lions sitting majestically on their gateposts beside the road to Henstridge. The old house is also associated with an intriguing ghost story. Some years before the demolition, the Marchioness of Anglesey, who owned the property, had left it empty and in the charge of an old housekeeper. One December she lent the house to a London friend and her children for a Christmas holiday on the understanding that they must do everything the housekeeper asked of them. Among other things, the housekeeper insisted that the family make a point of avoiding the entrance hall around 5pm on any afternoon. This was strictly adhered to for some time but one day the visitors had some other children round to play. Their departure was delayed and the lady found herself in the hall as the clock struck five.

'Hardly had the hour passed when her notice was attracted by a figure issuing from the door of one of the bedrooms on the first floor, which could be seen from the hall,' wrote the Victorian clergyman the Rev. W. S. Swayne in his history of Stalbridge, published in 1889. 'The figure was that of a woman enveloped in flames, who repeated to herself in an agonised voice: "I have done it. I have done it." The figure disappeared immediately into the door of another room.'

Climbing the stairs, Lady Anglesey's friend was surprised to find that the doors to both the room from which the woman had emerged and the one that she had entered were locked. Intrigued, she decided to be in the hall at 5pm on another day – and witnessed a repeat of the strange event. Following her return to London, the woman paid Lady Anglesey a visit and begged to know the story behind it. The Marchioness told her that some years earlier, the house was inhabited by a widowed mother and her only son, who was not yet of age. One day the boy announced that he had fallen in love with the gamekeeper's daughter. The mother reproved him for his indiscretion and ordered him never to mention the subject again. Not long after, the boy returned to the subject and announced his intention to marry the girl. Once more his mother refused to listen to him.

Some weeks later, the son broached the subject a third time. This time he told his mother it would be better for her to accept the inevitable, as the girl was already his wife and had been for several months. The mother was so indignant that she turned her son out of the house with orders never to return.

A few months later, the young man was delighted to receive a visit from his mother, who appeared to have had a change of heart and indicated that she was now willing to receive both him and his wife at Stalbridge House. The couple duly arrived and the beautiful young wife did her best to please her mother-in-law. All appeared to be going well until one evening, when the son arrived home from a day's hunting to be met with the news that his young wife had burned to death.

'The accident had occurred in this way,' wrote W. S. Swayne. 'His wife had entered her mother-in-law's dressing-room about 5 o'clock in the evening, ready dressed for dinner. The mother-in-law was sitting in a distant part of the room before the looking-glass and the girl stood before the fire. Suddenly the elder lady heard a scream and, turning, saw her daughter-in-law enveloped in flames, having accidentally caught her dress on fire from the hearth.'

The older woman's story was accepted without question – until the final day of her own life. As she lay on her deathbed, she confessed to her son that she had in fact murdered his young wife by pushing her into the fire. From that day on, Stalbridge House was haunted by the figure of the old woman enveloped in flames and proclaiming her crime. The haunting continued until 1822, when the house was knocked down, the fiery ghost laid and the old woman's tortured soul hopefully able to move on.

CHAPTER TWENTY-TWO

The Ghost in the Gallery

But for the strange events at Beaminster parish church in June 1728, John Daniel would be just another name in the burial register. His short life was punctuated by tragedy and ended in mysterious circumstances. But it's what happened in the weeks after his death that causes him to be remembered almost 300 years later.

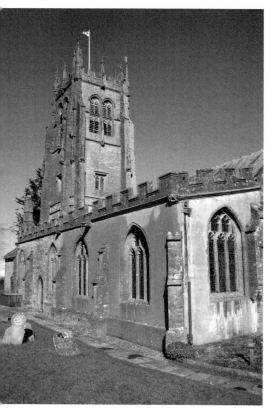

Beaminster church

John never knew his mother, Hannah, who died in October 1714, soon after he was born and two years after her marriage to his father, Isaac Daniel, a Beaminster smallholder. Isaac remarried in February 1717 and later that year his new wife, Elizabeth, who had previously been his servant, gave birth to another boy, Isaac Jnr.

As far as we know, the family lived happily enough until August 1726, when tragedy struck again. Isaac Snr became sick and died, unable to leave a will but orally conveying his last wishes to the necessary three witnesses. He left 5 shillings to each of his sons and the rest of his personal estate to Elizabeth. He also exercised his right to name the successors to his tenancy, nominating John to inherit 5 acres of pasture and one of arable and Isaac Jnr 8 acres of pasture and half-an-acre of arable.

Sadly, John enjoyed his little inheritance for less than two years. In May 1728, a few hours after being sent out by his stepmother to tend her cows, he was found dead on a small island in a stream 200 yards from home. He was thirteen. According to one contemporary account, his body was in an odd position and bore 'several black spots round his neck and on his breast and belly, which tokens of violence'. This caused 'no small stir' in the West Dorset town and aroused 'great suspicion' that he had been murdered. But there was no firm evidence and Elizabeth Daniel allayed people's fears by insisting that her stepson had suffered fits during his lifetime.

John was buried in St Mary's churchyard on 1 June 1728 without an inquest into the cause of death. And that is where the matter would probably have ended but for the happenings at the church three weeks later. These are independently described in two anonymous eighteenth-century documents – a handwritten account and a letter published in the *Gentleman's Magazine* forty-six years after John's death. The two documents are largely consistent but contain enough discrepancies to suggest they were written by different people, which strengthens the case for the story's authenticity.

Both reports tell how a dozen or so boys were playing ball in the churchyard after their Saturday lessons in the gallery, which doubled as a schoolroom. When three or four of them went back into the church to clean up, they heard a 'tingling noise', like the sound of a small bell or a brass pan being struck. The sound seemed to be getting closer and closer and they ran outside to tell their friends. They thought someone was trying to frighten them but when they investigated, there was no-one there. Descending the stairs from the gallery, they heard a second noise, 'as of a man going in great boots'. 'Terrified at that,' says the letter in the *Gentleman's Magazine*, they ran round the church, and when at the belfry or west door they heard a third noise, like a minister preaching, which was succeeded by another of a congregation singing psalms.'

Events became even more alarming when one boy saw the apparition of a white coffin with brass nails lying on a writing desk at the far end of the schoolroom. He was so shocked that he cried out and 'leapt or fell' down the stairs and bruised himself. The other boys headed up the stairs and the four or five who could see into the gallery from the doorway then 'saw the apparition of the above-mentioned John Daniel sitting at a writing desk, where he used to write when living'. He was in a writing posture and appeared to be wearing his school clothes and hat, which hung over his face. The boys also saw the coffin with its brass nails and a piece of tape or gartering attached to one of its handles.

The first to recognise John was his ten-year-old half-brother, who remarked: 'There sits our John, with just such a coat on as I have, with a pen in his hand and a book before him and a coffin by him.' The boys resumed their game in the churchyard but returned to the church from time to time and on each occasion saw the apparition again. Eventually Isaac Daniel threw a stone at the figure, saying, 'There, Johnny, take it.' Immediately the apparition vanished, leaving the church in a 'thick darkness' for two or three minutes.

This episode soon became the talk of Beaminster, fanning the flames of suspicion that had been simmering since John Daniel's unexplained death. Some of his relatives asked a magistrate to investigate. He separately questioned eight of the boys, aged nine to twelve, and was impressed at how much their stories tallied. One of them was regarded as especially reliable, being 'sober and sedate' and a newcomer to the school. Although he had never met John Daniel, he was able to give an 'exact description of the person of the deceased, and took notice of one thing in the apparition which escaped the others, viz a white cloth or rag which was bound round one of his hands. The woman who laid out the corpse for interment deposed, on oath, that she took such a white cloth from the hand, it being put on it a week or four days before his death, his hand being lame.'

Coroner George Filliter was sent for and ordered the exhumation of the body. As it was being raised, two of the boys who had seen the apparition but were not at John Daniel's funeral were heard to comment on the gartering on the coffin handle, just as they had seen it in the church. 'The sexton and all others that were present at the boy's burial did not remember that any such string or gartering was left in the handle of the coffin at the time it was laid in the grave,' says the handwritten account.

On 6 July, Mr Filliter belatedly opened an inquest at the King's Arms. It included the customary viewing of the body by the coroner and jury – a dubious experience, given it was the middle of summer and the body had been underground for six weeks. A surgeon was unable to say for certain whether there was any dislocation of the boy's neck. The jury were, however, told of the body's unusual posture when found and of the black or blue spots on the neck. Two women testified that when they saw the body two days after death, they noticed a strip of black cloth around the neck – an observation confirmed by the joiner who put the body in the coffin. The jury concluded that John Daniel had been strangled.

Despite this, there was deemed to be insufficient evidence to begin a prosecution although there was plenty of finger-pointing in Beaminster. The author of the handwritten document points out that John Daniel had been missing for a whole night before his body was found, yet his stepmother failed to initiate a search. This added to people's suspicions, as did a change in her deportment: before the boy's death, she was 'very gay, singing and merry' and 'has since affected to sing but it is observed by the neighbourhood that she pined away. Her lips wale, and in this time in an infirm way.' The document even implies that there may have been a motive for Elizabeth Daniel to kill her stepson, stating that not long before his death, John had nominated her to succeed him as the tenant of his part of his father's estate and hinting that he may have been bullied into it.

Even this was not the end of the story. Six weeks after the apparition of John Daniel, the congregation at a Wednesday morning service at St Mary's included a fourteen-year-old girl known for her truthfulness. The teenager was kneeling behind her master in the gallery when she saw a woman push open the door to the stairs and look up at the school area. The girl told her master there was a woman at the church door wishing to speak with him. The master, who had a sick child at home, feared that someone had come to tell him the child's condition had worsened and rushed down the stairs, only to see the door slam before him. He went outside but there was no-one there. He thoroughly searched the churchyard but again found no-one, which 'increased his surprise for that it was impossible for any human creature to get out of the churchyard in so short a time'.

The noise of the door closing violently had been heard by the minister and congregation and all were mystified, as there was no wind and no-one in a position to touch the door. The girl described the woman as being thin of stature, 'rosier with the pox' and with a pale countenance. She was wearing a 'sad' or dark-coloured gown, a flowered handkerchief around her neck and a straw hat. Those who heard this said it was a perfect description of Hannah Daniel's person and clothing at the time of her death in 1714. 'And it is to be observed,' notes the handwritten document, 'that the girl who saw her could not possibly describe her, being born about the time of her death.'

CHAPTER TWENTY-THREE
Smugglers in the Church

A t some point during the Napoleonic wars, an order went out for a peal of bells to be rung at St George's Church, Fordington, Dorchester, to celebrate a naval victory. Some sources claim Fordington was intended to be a link in a chain of churches stretching from Plymouth to London; others suggest the plan was for bellringers at all Dorchester's churches to ring a peal simultaneously. Either way, the plan was thwarted. Fordington's bells remained mysteriously silent and the ringers were accused of disloyalty to the Crown. The ringers were as mystified as everyone else – until someone went into the belfry to investigate and found a tub of smuggled brandy tied to each of the clappers.

Fordington was one of several Dorset churches used by smugglers to store their contraband in the eighteenth and early nineteenth centuries, when public sympathy lay almost entirely with the 'free-traders', as they

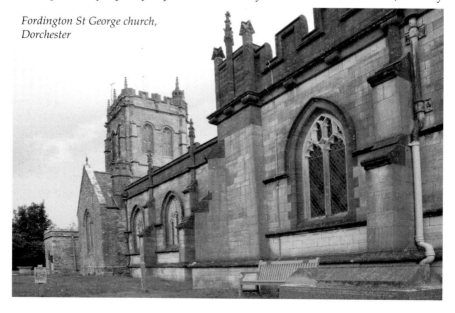

Fordington St George church, Dorchester

called themselves. Churches at Kinson, Owermoigne, Langton Matravers, Fleet and Stanton St Gabriel are all known to have been used for this purpose. J. Meade Falkner's classic children's adventure novel *Moonfleet* includes a description of brandy tubs bumping against each other as they bobbed around in the flooded vaults beneath the little church at Fleet

The surviving part of the old church at Fleet

during a service. The incident is thought to be based on a real event.

At Kinson on the outskirts of Bournemouth, St Andrew's is traditionally known as 'the Smugglers' Church'. Before the development of Bournemouth as a seaside resort in the nineteenth century, Kinson was a major smuggling centre whose residents included the legendary 'king of the smugglers', Isaac Gulliver. His many properties included elegant Howe Lodge in Brook Road, which was demolished in the 1950s; the forerunner of Kinson's present Pelhams community centre building; and Hillamsland Farm across the river at Longham.

Generations of smugglers stored their goods in Kinson church, both in the tower and in a chest tomb in the churchyard, which had a pivoted stone at one end to enable easy access. Over the years so many tubs of brandy were hauled up the tower that grooves were worn in the parapets by the ropes. The damage was not restored until the 1930s. Another memorial stone pays a shamelessly sympathetic tribute to the smuggler Robert Trotman, who was shot dead in a battle with the Royal Navy following a landing of contraband tea on Bournemouth beach in 1765. The inscription says that Trotman, from Rowde in Wiltshire, was 'barbarously Murder'd on the shore near Poole' and adds:

Robert Trotman's gravestone in Kinson churchyard

'A little Tea, one leaf I did not steal
For Guiltless Bloodshed I to GOD appeal.
Put Tea in one scale human Blood in tother
And think what tis to slay they harmless Brother.'

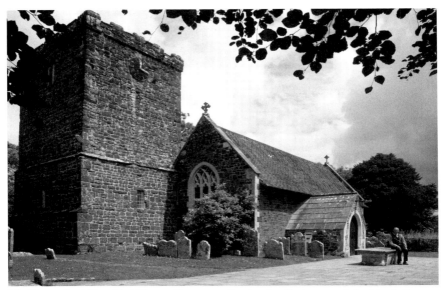

The 'Smugglers' Church' at Kinson, Bournemouth, showing the tower and chest tomb (far right) where generations of smugglers hid their contraband

Langton Matravers church was used for storing contraband

According to the Swanage historian William Masters Hardy, smuggled goods were regularly hidden under the church roof at Langton Matravers in the 1830s, most of the local smugglers' other hiding places already having been discovered by the Coastguard. Eventually word of the church's unholy usage reached the Collector of Customs at Poole, who paid Langton Matravers a surprise visit and seized a sizeable cargo. Hardy was not aware that Langton church was ever used by smugglers again but the diary of C. W. T. Dean makes it clear that it was.

Dean, born in 1859, was a grandson of Charles Hayward, a quarryman and smuggler at Langton Matravers. In a diary entry dated 1869, Dean recorded an incident at the parish church, which he described as his 'great adventures with Grandfather'. It was just after dusk when Grandfather posted the ten-year-old outside the church gate as a lookout. The boy was instructed not to stand still but to walk up and down and 'not to look too involved with anything in particular'. There was a cold wind blowing so he was more than happy to obey. Charles was further instructed that if a Peeler-policeman should happen to appear, he must alert his grandfather using a prearranged signal.

The diary goes on: 'Seven gentlemen arrived variously to meet my grandfather, and they all went inside the church. A Peeler came down from Garfield, past me and thence on to Stepps. I had given the alert (taking my cap off, shaking it and putting it on again) and whilst the Peeler walked by, all was silent in the church, nor any light. Presently came two stone carts from Garfield end, and the seven gentlemen came out and assisted the drivers with unloading the stones; these were stacked flat-down and not up-down. The men then brought in barrels of all sizes and different shapes. All together this went into the church – I could not see where, but I heard a bell make a half-sounding, and heard a man say something bad. They then, I think, came to the porch and the two drivers took papers from my grandfather and reloaded the stone and drove off to the Stepps. I heard much talking; my grandfather came out to me, thanked me profusely for my assistance, and gave me a gold coin. I went home, and straight to bed.'

Dean's story is one of the last recorded episodes from the eighteenth and nineteenth century heyday of smuggling in Dorset, which had all but died out by the 1860s following a period of free trade, which had removed most of the incentive to smuggle.

CHAPTER TWENTY-FOUR
The Sherborne Poisoner

Frederick Bryant may not have been the army's most eligible bachelor but it is not hard to see why Charlotte McHugh was attracted to him. Among other things the military policeman, serving with the Dorset Regiment, offered the unsophisticated Irish gypsy girl a tempting escape route from trouble-torn Londonderry in the years following the First World War. What Bryant saw in McHugh is more difficult to discern. She could not read, write or tell the time and was later described by her own legal representative as lacking beauty, dignity, charm or any other attraction.

Charlotte was still only nineteen in 1922, when she eloped with Fred, who was twenty-four and leaving the army after five years in Northern Ireland. In her words, she was expecting to find a 'place in the sun'. In reality she was merely exchanging poverty for poverty. After marrying in Somerset, the couple moved into a labourer's cottage at Nether Compton, near Sherborne, where they and their fast-growing family lived in squalor.

Charlotte Bryant

Charlotte sought consolation in the pub or by indulging her propensity for extravagance and taking a series of lovers. Known to some locals as Compton Liz and to others as Black Bess, she acquired a reputation for accepting drinks from strange men and then disappearing with them. If they went back to her cottage, her children would be sent out to buy sweets. For Charlotte, these liaisons were not only an enjoyable diversion but a way of supplementing her farm-labourer husband's meagre income. She became adept at extracting money from her men: one Yeovil businessman handed over £25 to pay for an abortion, only for Charlotte to reappear months later with a baby and a demand for more cash as the price of her silence.

Fred Bryant turned a blind eye on his wife's infidelity, telling a neighbour, 'Four pounds a week is better than 30 bob. I don't care a damn what she does.' He even became good friends with the last and most serious of her lovers, the horse-dealer and travelling salesman Leonard Parsons, also known as Bill Moss. Between 1933 and 1935, Parsons not only lived part-time at the Bryants' cottage but shared a razor with his lover's husband and drank with him at the Crown. Parsons was also the undisputed father of Charlotte's fifth and youngest child.

Parsons was staying at the cottage in May 1935, when Fred Bryant suffered the first in a series of mysterious illnesses. A neighbour found him sitting on the stairs, groaning and shuddering and clutching his stomach. By the time Dr McCarthy arrived, he had cramp in his legs and severe diarrhoea and was vomiting green froth. The doctor diagnosed food poisoning. Fred made a full recovery but fell ill again with similar symptoms three months later. This time gastroenteritis was diagnosed.

In October 1935, the family moved to Coombe on the outskirts of Sherborne. Meanwhile Charlotte was feeling increasingly insecure about her relationship with Parsons and took various steps to try and stop him leaving. These included hiding his clothes and warning a garage owner not to repair his car on the grounds that he would not be able to pay. She even twice hired a car and driver to take her to a gypsy camp near Weston-super-Mare to show her baby to Parsons' long-term lover Priscilla Loveridge, the mother of four of his children. Loveridge seemed unsurprised and unmoved, later describing Parsons as 'a woman's fancy man'.

Fred Bryant's final illness began on 10 December when he was hauling stone in a quarry at the farm where he worked. Eleven days later he was no better, telling a neighbour, Mrs Stone: 'The pain is awful. It's driving me mad. It burns me inside like a red-hot poker. I'm dying. I'm sure I'm going to die.'

His wife was consistently unsympathetic. She told Mrs Stone: 'I haven't got Fred insured but he could have a military funeral.'

At noon on 22 December, Bryant was finally admitted to the Yeatman Hospital, Sherborne, where he died less than three hours later, aged thirty-nine. Dr McCarthy was suspicious enough not to issue a death certificate. It occurred to him that his patient's symptoms – diarrhoea, vomiting, stomach pains, leg cramps and dragging legs – were typical of arsenic poisoning. After the second of two post-mortem examinations, Bryant's internal organs were sent in sealed jars to a Home Office analyst, whose report several days later confirmed arsenic as the cause of death.

By this time Dorset police had called in Scotland Yard, who sealed off the Bryants' cottage at Coombe and sent Charlotte and her five children to the public assistance institution at Sturminster Newton. Detectives visited every chemist in the area to check their poison registers and also Yeovil's glove factories, where red arsenic was used in the manufacturing process. One Yeovil pharmacist remembered selling a tin of Eureka weedkiller, which contained arsenic, to an illiterate woman who signed the register with a cross. This was on 21 December, the day before Bryant's death, when his wife left the cottage for three hours to collect what proved to be his last bottle of medicine.

As well as Charlotte Bryant, neighbour Lucy Ostler also found herself under suspicion after nursing Fred in his dying days. The widowed mother-of-seven initially made a statement that she had no knowledge of the cause of his death. Faced with the possibility of a murder charge, however, she made a second statement in which she recalled waking at 3am to hear Charlotte coaxing Fred to drink what she said was Oxo. Minutes later Fred was vomiting and twelve hours after that he died. Soon after his death, Charlotte pointed to a green tin in a cupboard and told Mrs Ostler: 'I must get rid of that.' The description of the tin matched that of the Eureka weedkiller. Mrs Ostler also talked of finding a burnt tin of the same size when she was raking out the ashes under the Bryants' boiler. Police later recovered this in the yard.

Soon after making this statement, Lucy Ostler was released from custody and Charlotte Bryant charged with murdering her husband by arsenic poisoning. She was sobbing as she left Sturminster Newton for her first court appearance in Sherborne.

Her four-day trial at the Dorset Assizes in Dorchester began on 27 May 1936 before a packed courtroom, including a full contingent of Fleet Street reporters. As well as Lucy Ostler and Priscilla Loveridge, witnesses included Leonard Parsons, who said Charlotte had, more than once, asked him to marry her, saying she would 'soon be a widow'. He denied he had ever brought weedkiller into the house but he did remember an occasion when Fred Bryant found a tin on a shelf and was told by his wife that it was weedkiller. Charlotte herself also took the stand, denying that she ever had weedkiller in the house.

Controversially, the defence called Fred and Charlotte's two eldest children, Ernest, aged thirteen, and ten-year-old Lily to give evidence. Lily's red beret was scarcely higher than the top of the witness box; Ernest fought bravely but in vain to hold back the tears, which rolled down his cheeks on to his collar and suit as he told how his mother had asked him to throw some bottles away before Christmas.

If the appearance of Ernest and Lily was designed to elicit sympathy from the jury, it appears to have failed: they took just one hour to find Charlotte guilty. As the judge pronounced the inevitable death sentence, the prisoner let out a shuddering moan, which broke the silence of the courtroom. She almost fell but was caught by a wardress. 'Not guilty,' she whispered between sobs as she clung to the rail, a tragic, broken figure, crouched and shivering. Her piteous sobbing could still be heard as she was led from the courtroom.

Charlotte Bryant was hanged at Exeter Prison on 15 July 1936, telling her solicitor the previous day: 'I am ready to meet my maker.' In her will she left her estate of 5 shillings 8.5 pence (29p) to be divided between her five children. Two days later the youngsters were adopted by the Dorset Public Assistance Committee and the family split up.

During the trial and for seventy-six years after it, Leonard Parsons was the only one of Charlotte Bryant's many lovers to be publicly identified. But in an article for the *Blackmore Vale Magazine* in 2012, I was able to publish details of another – Benjamin Bowen, who lived at Adber in the neighbouring

Benjamin Bowen, one of Charlotte Bryant's other lovers

parish of Trent. His granddaughter, Jan Ridout, told me: 'He worked as a gardener and supplied Charlotte with weedkiller. We don't know if he knew he was supplying it for that reason. But about that time he moved from Adber to Mudford so they never caught up with him.' The connection was naturally hushed up by Bowen's family. He died in 1972.

CHAPTER TWENTY-FIVE

The Other Father of Evolution

Almost everyone has heard of Charles Darwin but relatively few even know the name of Alfred Russel Wallace. Yet in the view of some, this former resident of Broadstone deserves as much credit as the man we think of as the 'Father of Evolution'. The late Dorset writer Rodney Legg went so far as to describe Wallace as 'the man who could have been Darwin'. In fact, Wallace and Darwin were not only contemporaries of a like mind but

Alfred Russel Wallace

collaborators who jointly published a pamphlet based on their shared thoughts on the theory of evolution. Called *On the Tendency of Species to Form Varieties*, it was published in 1858 and only two copies are known to survive.

That is the traditional version of the event. But Wallace supporters claim it was he who first prepared the historic paper on the 'survival of the fittest' – and that had he sent it to a scientific journal, he rather than Darwin would today be a household name. Instead Wallace sent his paper to Darwin himself, plunging his fellow naturalist into consternation. Darwin had been working on a similar theory for twenty years and was now in danger of being pipped at the post. The solution, suggested by a friend and fellow scientist, was to present both men's work as a joint paper – which they did but without Wallace's permission. Wallace appears never to have resented this, however, and remained a friend and correspondent of his more famous collaborator for the rest of his life.

Wallace, born in Monmouthshire in 1823, became interested in geology and fossils at an early age and taught himself botany and the rudiments of classification while still in his teens. Inspired by the accounts of Humbolt and Darwin of their respective travels in South America, he and his friend Henry Bates, who collected beetles, decided to go to the Amazon as collectors. They arrived in Brazil in 1848 and Wallace made extensive notes about the flora and fauna, geology and rainfall as well as mapping rivers and measuring altitude by taking the boiling point of water with a sensitive thermometer.

'I saw a large monkey looking down at me, and seeming as much astonished as I was myself,' he wrote of one encounter. 'I should have liked to have had a good look at him, but he thought it safer to retreat. The next day we heard a whole troop approaching and we therefore hid ourselves under some trees, and with guns cocked, and awaited their coming. At last one approached too near for its safety. Mr Leavens fired, and it fell, the rest making off with all possible speed.'

Touchingly, Wallace commented: 'The poor little creature was not quite dead, and its cries, its innocent-looking countenance and delicate little hands were quite childlike.' In the very next sentence he added: 'Having often heard how good monkey was, I took it home and had it cut up and fried for breakfast. There was about as much of it as a fowl, and the meat resembled rabbit, without any very peculiar or unpleasant flavour.'

On another occasion Wallace came face to face with a large black cat. 'As it moved slowly on, and its whole body and long curving tail came into full view in the middle of the road, I saw that it was a fine black jaguar,' he said. He involuntarily raised his gun to his shoulder, then remembered that it was loaded with small shot, which would only have wounded the animal. Before disappearing into the thicket, the jaguar stood for a moment looking at Wallace, who was too thrilled to be terrified. 'I had at length had a full view, in his native wilds, of the rarest variety of the most powerful and dangerous animal inhabiting the American continent,' he observed.

Wallace left South America on the brig' *Helen* in July 1852 along with countless crates packed with notes and specimens of flora and fauna, plus a number of live animals. Tragically, three weeks into the Atlantic, the *Helen* was engulfed by fire and Wallace had to watch from a lifeboat as the results of four years' work were destroyed, including all but one of the living creatures, the sole survivor being a parrot. Wallace and the crew of the Helen survived for nine days in their leaky boats before being picked up by a vessel sailing from Cuba to London. Two years later he was on his way to the

Malay Archipelago, where he spent eight years and collected a staggering 125,000 specimens. It was during his absence that the 'joint' paper was published.

Several of the birds and insects that Wallace discovered were named after him, as was Wallace's Line, which divides the flora and fauna of Asia from those of Australasia. Wallace even lived for a time with Dyak head-hunters. After feasting in their long house, he noted: 'Slept very comfortably with half-a-dozen smoke-dried human skulls suspended over my head.'

Wallace possessed one of the greatest minds of his generation and used it in a variety of ways. He was a prolific writer, responsible for an impressive and varied list of titles, ranging from *Travels on the Amazon* to *Is Mars Inhabitable*?

The fossil memorial to Alfred Russel Wallace in Broadstone churchyard

'He wrote to make an honest bob and was quite happy to write on any subject,' his grandson, John Wallace, of Bournemouth, once told me. 'He was even one of four people asked to comment on whether Shakespeare or Bacon wrote the works attributed to Shakespeare. I don't suppose he really knew but he was quite happy to write about it.'

Unlike Darwin, Wallace also had a very readable writing style, which most people could understand. His place as one of the world's leading naturalists was officially recognised in 1910, when he was awarded the Order of Merit. He had moved to Parkstone, Poole, in 1889 and, seven years later, to Broadstone, where he spent his last eleven years. He built a house called Old Orchard – since demolished – in what is now Wallace Road and created a fine garden stocked with unusual shrubs and trees. He died in 1913, aged ninety, and was buried in Broadstone Cemetery, where his grave is marked by a 7ft fossilised tree trunk from Portland. There is also a memorial plaque in Westminster Abbey.

Coincidentally, Dorset also has a direct association with Darwin, who spent a month in Bournemouth with his family in the summer of 1862. They rented two cottages in the Victorian health resort when one of his sons and then his wife contracted scarlet fever. Darwin himself stayed at Cliff Cottage, a quaintly attractive thatched dwelling, which had stood on the West Cliff since about 1815.

Darwin may have been impressed by Bournemouth's qualities as a health resort but the place did little to stimulate his fertile brain. 'I do nothing except look at a few flowers, and there are very few here, for the country is wonderfully barren,' he wrote to his friend Lord Avebury. To fellow botanist J. D. Hooker, he commented: 'This is nice but barren country and I can find nothing to look at. Even the brooks and ponds produce nothing. The country is like Patagonia. My wife is almost well, thank God, and soon home.'

Cliff Cottage was demolished in 1876 and replaced by two large apartment houses which were later amalgamated to become first the Southcliff Tower and later the Regent Palace Hotel. This in turn was knocked down in 1981 to make way for the Bournemouth International Centre.

CHAPTER TWENTY-SIX
Farmer Jesty's 'Quantum Leap'

Buried in a Purbeck churchyard are the remains of farmer whose name occupies an unlikely niche in the annals of medical history. Benjamin Jesty is described on his gravestone at Worth Matravers as an 'upright and honest man, particularly noted for having been the first person (known) that introduced the Cow Pox by inoculation'. Jesty's wife, Elizabeth, and sons Robert and Benjamin Jnr also deserve some credit, for they were the human guinea-pigs who braved his experiments with a stocking needle in 1774 – twenty-two years before the far more famous Edward Jenner administered similar treatment in another part of southern England. Just as Alfred Russel Wallace is often called 'the man who could have been Darwin', we might equally well refer to Jesty as 'the man who could have been Jenner'.

Although Benjamin and Elizabeth spent their later years at Worth Matravers, it was at another village on the other side of Dorset that Jesty carried out his experiment. The young family lived in a farmhouse called

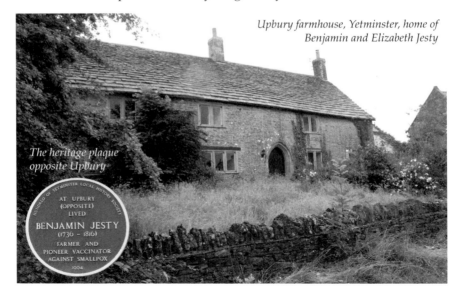

Upbury farmhouse, Yetminster, home of Benjamin and Elizabeth Jesty

The heritage plaque opposite Upbury

HUNDRED OF YETMINSTER LOCAL HISTORY SOCIETY
AT UPBURY
(OPPOSITE)
LIVED
BENJAMIN JESTY
(1736 – 1816)
FARMER AND
PIONEER VACCINATOR
AGAINST SMALLPOX
1994

Upbury in his native village of Yetminster, near Sherborne, where Jesty followed in his father's footsteps as a farmer. Elizabeth came from the neighbouring village of Longburton.

The couple's background in the farming community would have made them aware of the folklore that people who had had contact with cows that had cowpox appeared to be immune to the related but far more serious smallpox virus. Whereas smallpox usually led to facial scarring and often death, those with cowpox escaped with a mild fever and lesions on the hands at the point where the virus entered the skin. Dairymaids were also known for their fair complexions, in contrast to smallpox survivors. Jesty had first-hand evidence of this through his dairymaids, Anne Notley and Mary Reade. Both had been infected with cowpox by contact with the udders of cows they had milked yet both escaped smallpox even when nursing relatives with the disease.

When a smallpox epidemic broke out in the area in the spring of 1774, Jesty made what his biographer, Patrick J. Pead, describes as a 'quantum leap in thinking'. 'Faced with the awful implications of his family suffering the ravages of smallpox, and knowing the hazards of inoculation, he conceived an ingenious idea,' writes Pead. Inoculation had been practised in Britain for several decades but it involved introducing one of the actual smallpox viruses. This saved many lives but claimed others due to a lack of control over the type of virus used. Jesty's 'quantum leap' was to borrow the inoculation method but replace the smallpox virus with cowpox.

Such was Jesty's confidence in his plan that he took his family to Chetnole, where his neighbour William Elford had some cows grazing that he knew had the marks of cowpox on their udders. He then used a stocking needle to take a tiny sample of material from a lesion on an udder and inserted it into his wife's arm just below the elbow. He then repeated the procedure with Robert and Benjamin, then aged just three and two respectively, but omitted baby Betty.

Jesty's effort may never have become known had it not been for a complication that arose. While the infant boys suffered no significant ill-effects, Elizabeth's arm became inflamed and her husband summoned medical help. Dr Trowbridge from Cerne Abbas told him: 'You have done a bold thing but I will get you through if I can.' Elizabeth was treated for a fever, made a full recovery and never contracted smallpox. Her boys also avoided the disease, despite being inoculated with a smallpox virus by Dr Trowbridge in 1789, when both were in their late teens.

Although Jesty did his best to keep a low-profile, his actions became widely known in the local community, which proved decidedly unsympathetic. Suspicious of anything that did not conform to their existing

Worth Matravers church   *Benjamin Jesty's grave at Worth Matravers*

beliefs and familiar with biblical warnings against contaminating the body with animal matter, people subjected him to physical and verbal abuse. Despite this, Jesty continued farming at Yetminster and carrying out his parish duties as an Overseer of the Poor and a member of the Yetminster Vestry. It was not until 1796 that Jesty – now a father of seven – moved his family to Downshay Manor, Harmans Cross, near Swanage, a tenancy that offered more land than Upbury and more space for his growing family.

Coincidentally, 1796 was also the year in which Edward Jenner first administered a cowpox vaccination, although the seeds for this were probably sown twenty-five to thirty years earlier during a conversation with a dairymaid in his native Gloucestershire, where he was apprenticed to an apothecary. He also studied medicine privately under a London surgeon before returning to Berkeley, the parish of his birth, in 1773 to work as a general practitioner. His duties included inoculation of the smallpox virus and it did not escape his attention that many members of the farming community failed to react and when questioned confirmed that they had contracted cowpox at some point in the past.

As often happens with innovative ideas that surface in more than one place at the same time, Jenner's thoughts about vaccination were running parallel to Jesty's albeit from a different background. He made notes about his theories and shared his ideas with his medical friends, although with a couple of notable exceptions, they were generally discouraging. Jenner was reluctant to put his professional reputation on the line and waited twenty years before acting on his theory. On 14 May 1796, he used a surgeon's lancet to transfer matter from a cowpox lesion on a dairymaid's hand to the arm of an eight-year-old boy, James Phipps. Six weeks later he inoculated James with smallpox but the boy was unaffected. In 1798 he took his experiments a step further, first transferring cowpox from a cow's udder to another boy, then carrying out human-to-human transfers of matter to at least six other children, two of whom were subsequently inoculated with smallpox and again were unaffected. Jenner then published his findings and in doing so coined the phrase 'variolae vaccinae' – literally 'smallpox of the cow'. This is the origin of the word 'vaccine', which we use today.

Jenner opted to forgo the chance to amass a personal fortune for his work, instead making it freely available in Britain and abroad (his original report was translated into six languages within three years). He was, however, honoured my many countries, including Britain, where the Government awarded him £10,000 in 1802 and £20,000 in 1807.

Jesty, meanwhile, was regularly vaccinating locals at Worth Matravers, who clearly showed a level of faith in the method that had been lacking at Yetminster two decades earlier. There is even a memorial inside Worth Matravers church to someone whose mother 'was personally inoculated for the cow pox by Benjamin Jesty of Downshay'. Among Jesty's greatest supporters was a Swanage clergyman, the Rev. Dr Andrew Bell, who campaigned to get some recognition for a man who was 'so often forgotten by those who have heard of Dr Jenner'. As a result, in 1805 he was invited to the Vaccine Pock Institution in London, where he was questioned in great detail by the organisation's members, who also tested his and Robert Jesty's continued immunity by inoculating them with live smallpox.

The meeting finally earned Benjamin public recognition from the medical profession, whose representatives praised not only his pioneering work but his 'superior strength of mind' in the face of 'prevailing popular prejudices' and the 'clamorous reproaches of his neighbours'. The Institution also presented Jesty with a testimonial scroll, a pair of gold-mounted lancets and 15 guineas to cover his expenses. It also commissioned a portrait of him by leading painter Michael W. Sharp, whose other subjects included the Duke of Wellington. The oil painting returned to the Jesty family for a few years in the mid-nineteenth century but had not been heard of since 1888, when it was in the home of Frank Ezekiel Pope, a great-grandson of Benjamin Jesty.

Thanks to some impressive detective work, however, Patrick Pead tracked the lost portrait to South Africa in 2004, when it was owned by Charles Pope, a great-great-great nephew of Frank Ezekiel Pope. It has since been acquired and restored by the Wellcome Trust in London and in 2009 was loaned to the Dorset County Museum to be publicly exhibited for the first time since 1805.

Benjamin Jesty died in 1816 aged seventy-nine. His wife lived to the then advanced age of eighty-four. Sons Robert and Benjamin died in 1839 and 1838 respectively. Seven years before his death, Robert met the geologist Gideon Mantell, who noted in his journal that he 'informed me his name was Jesty, that his father practised vaccination as early as Dr Jenner, and that he himself was the first person ever vaccinated intentionally'.

Edward Jenner died in 1823 aged seventy-three, his place in medical history more firmly cemented than Jesty's, although Jenner himself had cited the Dorset farmer's work as corroborative evidence supporting his own. Jesty, however, has belatedly and deservedly gained an increasing amount of posthumous recognition in recent years.

The portrait of Benjamin Jesty, rediscovered after more than 100 years. Picture: Wellcome Trust

CHAPTER TWENTY-SEVEN
The Pulpit with Bullet Holes

Like thousands of other pulpits around the country, the early seventeenth-century timber structure at Abbotsbury parish church has provided a platform for generations of clergymen as they preached the word of God. But the oak pulpit in St Nicholas' church has one unique and incongruous feature – two holes made by musket balls fired in anger during the English Civil War. The holes in turn hint at a great and tragic drama that unfolded here more than 370 years ago.

Although the execution of King Charles I was still four-and-a-half years away, the first of the three main conflicts which made up the Civil War was already in full swing when a large contingent of Parliamentary troops marched on Abbotsbury in November 1644. Their aim was to rid the coastal village of its Royalist garrison, commanded by Colonel James Strangways, a son of Sir John Strangways, one of the King's most loyal supporters. The Strangways family mansion had already been occupied and ransacked by a detachment of Parliamentary troops eighteen months earlier, but this time the force was larger and more determined.

Some Royalists had taken refuge in the church, which became the first target of the Parliamentary commander, Sir Anthony Ashley Cooper, of Wimborne St Giles. The pulpit acquired its battle scars when Ashley Cooper's men fired through the church's north windows. What happened to those within is unclear but this was only the opening skirmish of a battle that went on for

Musket ball holes in the pulpit canopy at Abbotsbury church

more than six hours.

Having taken the church, Ashley Cooper invited Colonel Strangways to surrender. He refused. What followed was later described by one of the attackers as 'as hot a storm as ever I heard of'. In order to reach the main house, the Parliamentarians first had to burn down a small gatehouse. Ashley Cooper himself described what happened next: 'Our men rushed in through the fire and got into the hall porch, where with furze faggots they set fire on it, and plied the windows so hard with small shot that the enemy durst not appear in the low rooms.'

While this was happening, a second group of Parliamentary troops attacked the other side of the house using guns, fireballs, grenades and scaling ladders. They were hoping to set light to the second storey but were initially unsuccessful. Using iron bars, they instead prised open the windows and threw in blazing faggots of furze. Soon the house was well alight and the garrison had no choice but to surrender.

Wiser attackers might have stopped at this point but the Parliamentary men were in no mood for restraint. Ignoring warnings that Royalists' powder barrels could explode at any time, dozens of them stormed the building in search of plunder. And many paid with their lives. Only fifteen Parliamentary troops had been killed or wounded by their enemies but Ashley Cooper himself estimated that more than four times as many perished when the barrels went up.

The house itself was burned to the ground. The vast majority of Abbotsbury's monastic records and charters were also destroyed. Colonel James Strangways escaped to France but his father and elder brother, Colonel Giles Strangways, were captured after the Siege of Sherborne the following year and imprisoned in the Tower of London. Sir John was released three years later on the grounds of 'age and infirmities'. Giles was kept hostage and eventually released after his family paid a £10,000 fine. The total cost of the family's support for the Crown was £35,000. It has been estimated that this is the equivalent of £20 million in today's money.

Despite this, the Strangways family remained 100 per cent loyal to the Crown. When Charles II was in hiding before escaping to France following the Battle of Worcester, Giles gave him £100 – a contribution later described as 'the most seasonable present the royal fugitive ever received'.

CHAPTER TWENTY-EIGHT
Cromwell and the Clubmen

In August 1645, a few months after the bloodshed at Abbotsbury, another drama unfolded on a hill in the north of the county. For some time resentment had been building among the ordinary people of Dorset and other southern counties over the predations of both sides in the Civil War. For three years they had seen their crops destroyed and their livestock plundered. Their feelings were summed up in the opening lines of a published verse called *The Western Husbandman's Lamentation*:

> I had six oxen the other day
> And them the Roundheads fetched away
> A mischief be their speed.
> And had six horses left me whole
> And them the Cavalieros stole
> We poor men be agreed.

Several Roundhead soldiers were killed in February 1645 after villagers at Godmanstone, north of Dorchester, turned on them. Next day almost 1000 men gathered with guns and clubs and threatened to resist the French and Irish among the Cavaliers. Similar episodes were soon to happen in Sussex, Hampshire, Wiltshire, Berkshire, Somerset, Gloucestershire and the Welsh borders.

In Dorset, the Clubmen, as they are often called, were growing in number and becoming more organised. A committee was formed in each parish, weapons and ammunition were stockpiled and preparations were made to ring church bells to warn of soldiers approaching. The Clubmen spanned the social spectrum and included craftsmen, clergymen, lawyers and gentry as well as farmers and labourers. One obviously biased observer described them as a 'disorderly rabble and rude company of mongrel malignants and rotten-headed nauseous neutrals'. The Clubmen had no uniforms but wore white silk ribbons in their hats and carried banners with slogans such as 'Peace and Truth'.

On 12 May, 3000 gathered between Shaftesbury and Blandford and sent a letter listing their grievances to Colonel John Bingham, the Roundhead governor of Poole. He promised to investigate. Two weeks later 4000 gathered at Badbury Rings, near Wimborne, 'armed with clubs, swords, bills, pitchforks and other several weapons'. Their spokesman Thomas Young – an attorney described as 'more eloquent than honest' – read out declarations about 'our ancient laws and liberties' being 'altogether swallowed up in the arbitrary power of the sword' and agreeing to 'join with and assist one another in the mutual defence of our liberties and properties against all plunderers and all other unlawful violence whatsoever'.

More incidents followed but events reached a head at Hambledon Hill, between Child Okeford and Shroton, at the beginning of August 1645. Prompted by Oliver Cromwell's arrest of several leading Clubmen at Shaftesbury on 2 August, between 2000 and 4000 took up positions on the ancient hillfort to await his arrival. At the foot of the hill Cromwell met a musketeer, who said he was on his way to join the 'club army'. 'Being required to lay down his arms, he said he would first lose his life, but was not so good as his word, for though he cocked and presented his musket, he was prevented, disarmed and wounded but not killed.

Cromwell asked to speak to the Clubmen in peace only for his men to be shot at. He also asked them to lay down their arms but their commander, the Rev. Thomas Bravell, Rector of Compton Abbas, ordered them to refuse and threatened to shoot the first man to run away. Cromwell later described Bravell as one of two 'vile ministers' who were among the ringleaders.

The Clubmen were posted behind one of the prehistoric fortress's defensive banks to defend the pass to it, which was barely wide enough for three horses abreast. Cromwell ordered his troops to charge but they were quickly repelled with the loss of two killed, eight or nine wounded and six or seven horses slain. Major General Desborough then led Cromwell's regiment of horse around the ledge of the hill to enter from the rear. Despite their strategic advantage, the poorly-trained and ill-equipped Clubmen were no match for these professional soldiers. Within an hour Desborough had opened up the pass and disarmed and dispersed the Clubmen. Cromwell estimated that no more than a dozen Clubmen died in the encounter but another report puts the number of fatalities as high as sixty. All agree that many were wounded and that others escaped by 'sliding and tumbling down that great steep hill to the hazard of their necks'. Between 300 and 400 were taken prisoner, many of them, according to Cromwell, 'poor silly creatures, whom if you please to let me send home, they promise to be very dutiful for time to come, and will be hanged before they come out again'. Also taken were twelve colours and 600 guns but no ammunition. One of the colours bore the slogan: 'If you offer to plunder or take our cattle, Be assured we will bid you battle'.

The prisoners spent an uncomfortable night in Shroton church, which was turned into a temporary jail. But Cromwell was in a merciful mood and the following day, after having their names taken and listening to a lecture as to their future behaviour, the majority were released. The ringleaders were held a little longer for questioning. They included four clergymen, described as 'malignant priests, who were the principal stirrers up of the people to these tumultuous assemblies'. Among them were Thomas Bravell and the Vicar of Milton Abbas, John Talbot.

Another account suggests that thirteen of Cromwell's troops died on Hambledon Hill, including a Major Paltison. Sixteen were captured by the Clubmen and threatened with hanging but later freed.

CHAPTER TWENTY-NINE

Manston's Unique Place in History

The North Dorset village of Manston has an unusual claim to historical fame as the place that pioneered the modern practice of cremating the dead. But its role placed the rural community near Sturminster Newton at the very heart of a nationwide controversy more than 130 years ago. It also caused alarm among villagers, some of whom complained of 'very disagreeable odours' that were 'palpable enough to all who happened to be in the way of the wind'. Others considered the practice distasteful and possibly illegal. Some asserted that it 'interfered with the resurrection of the body'.

The mausoleum at Manston House, where bodies were stored to await the historic first cremations

Historically, cremation was practised by many ancient civilisations, including the Romans and the Saxons, but after the Anglo-Saxon era it died out in Britain. The flame of interest was rekindled in the nineteenth century and fanned by the immense pressure on cemetery space resulting from rapid population growth. In some cemeteries in Victorian London, bodies were buried up to fourteen deep. In 1874 the London surgeon, writer and painter Henry Thompson launched the Cremation Society, whose high-profile founder members included the novelist Anthony Trollope, the painter John Millais and the illustrator of *Alice in Wonderland*, John Tenniel. The society built its own crematorium at Woking,

Surrey, and in 1879 cremated a large horse. Although no-one could find anything illegal in this, the Home Secretary gave in to public pressure and banned any human cremations.

The campaign may well have ended there but for the interest of Captain Thomas Hanham, of Manston House, youngest son of the late Rev. Sir James Hanham, of Dean's Court, Wimborne. Captain Hanham's third wife, Edith, and his mother, Lady Eliza, who died in 1876 and 1877 respectively, had both expressed their wish to be cremated. For the next few years, Captain Hanham stored the women's bodies in a domed mausoleum, which survives to this day a stone's throw from Manston House. Their wooden coffins were kept inside lead coffins to comply with sanitation laws.

Captain Hanham eventually built his own crematorium nearby and on 8 October 1882 Mrs Edith Hanham, who had died of cancer, became the first person in modern Britain to be legally cremated. The following day Lady Hanham, who was eighty-nine when she died, became the second person to have her remains disposed of in this way.

Among those attending the two ceremonies was William Robinson, another cremation campaigner. 'Captain Hanham, respecting these [the women's] wishes, determined to carry them out in the face of all difficulties,' he wrote. 'These are numerous owing to the fact that no public body exists in this kingdom which carries out cremation, and those who desire to execute the wishes of their relations in such a case were driven to seek the means in foreign countries, at an amount of trouble and expense which made it impossible for most.'

Robinson added: 'The cremations were carried out in a simple and inexpensive furnace, not only without any nuisance to the neighbourhood but without the slightest unpleasantness to those who stood within two feet of the white flame, which promptly resolved the bodies to their harmless elements. The coffins, lead and all, were placed in the furnace on fire-brick and iron plates, which allowed the flames to rise freely up but prevented the ashes from falling to the furnace below.'

Robinson and other advocates of cremation claimed it was the only method of disposal that was free from danger to the living and avoided pollution of earth, air and water. In a letter to a local newspaper, the campaigner continued: 'The difficulty of detecting poisoning – the only objection to cremation which needs remark – is to be met by scientific testimony as to the cause of death, precautions being taken by not permitting cremation in cases where there is room for suspicion of foul play.'

Sturminster Newton's Medical Officer of Health, Dr Comyns Leach, was also present at the cremations and raised no objection. But they caused an outcry elsewhere. Duncan Skrine, of Reading, who described himself as the 'husband of Lady Hanham's favourite grandchild', called the cremations a 'revolting proceeding'. 'The grandchildren are unutterably shocked at the deed and the heartless publicity given to it,' he said. 'We are certain that Lady Hanham, the widow of a clergyman, thoroughly English in her sentiments, never could have contemplated, nor would have sanctioned, such a disposition of her remains.'

Skrine's comments brought a sharp rebuke from Captain Hanham. A little over a year later, however, the former Royal Navy officer himself passed away aged fifty-eight. He too was cremated at Manston on 4 December 1883 and the ceremony was historic for a second reason, as it was the first entirely Masonic funeral in England for 100 years. Mr Montague Guest, MP, of Canford Manor, near Wimborne, led the service. The mourners included Lord Portman's agent, James Forrester, whose wife, Julietta, described the occasion in her diary and hinted at the controversy surrounding it and her own abhorrence.

'Anthems were sung and the service commenced in the hall,' Julietta wrote. 'The corpse, followed by masons and others, then proceeded to the mausoleum, where other prayers, singing etc followed. At the conclusion each mason deposited his sprig of acacia, which he wore, on the coffin. The church, meantime, was locked up and the Rector away, he not agreeing with the late Captain's views nor with this style of funeral. Then a luncheon was partaken of at which about 100 sat down. Before leaving James inspected the crematorium, a structure near the house built under the supervision of Capt Hanham for his own cremation and that of others who might wish to follow his example. The public were not aware that the Captain's body was so soon to be reduced to ashes and went away under the impression that the event would not take place for a day or two. At about 8 this evening the coffin was placed in position and the fires lit. In less than two hours in the presence of the stepson, who according to ancient Greek custom had lighted the funeral pile, other friends and one or two doctors, cremation was declared by Dr Comyns Leach (who conducted the cremation) to have been most satisfactorily performed. So ended a shockingly anti-Christian ceremony.'

The Manston cremations effectively gave the practice a toehold in England and directly influenced later developments. In 1884 an eighty-four-year-old Welsh physician and Druid called William Price was tried for cremating his five-month-old son, whom he had named Jesus Christ Price. The judge could find nothing illegal in his actions and Price successfully sued for wrongful arrest, although he was awarded only a farthing in damages. Three more cremations followed at Woking the following year and the Cremation Society went on to open crematoria in Manchester in 1892,

Glasgow in 1895, Liverpool in 1896 and Darlington in 1901. London's world famous Golders Green followed in 1902 and Birmingham in 1903. By 1904, when Golders Green hosted the cremation of Cremation Society founder Sir Henry Thompson, more than 4400 people had had their remains reduced to ashes since the Hanhams of Manston started the trend twenty-two years earlier.

CHAPTER THIRTY
Monty Dined Here

When fire swept through the World's End on 9 February 1991, Dorset lost more than an ancient and picturesque pub. The thatched hostelry just off the A31 at Almer was not only a listed building dating back to the sixteenth century but had a history to match. Its beams were said to include timbers salvaged from the Spanish Armada; its eighteenth-century customers included smugglers and highwaymen; and in the twentieth century it developed strong links with the Royal Navy, whose sailors found the World's End a convenient place to break their overland journeys between the ports of Plymouth and Portsmouth. The stable bar displayed an impressive collection of cap tallies, ships' crests and other memorabilia, with a fair proportion of the British fleet represented. Thousands of servicemen and women had also signed their names on the walls.

The World's End before the 1991 fire

Most of this went up on smoke in 1991, when sparks from a chimney set light to the thatch and the building was gutted. At the time it was reported that the ultimate jewel in the pub's historical crown had also been lost. This was a framed letter relating to a legend that the 1944 D-Day invasion of Europe was planned at the World's End. A postwar landlord had been happy to feed the story to a nostalgia-hungry public after the Second World War. Guidebook writers also picked up the tale while passing coach drivers added it to the commentaries given to their passengers.

'I certainly get the impression that the immediate postwar landlord did his best to cash in on the story,' a more recent licensee, Roy McBeath, told me in 1984. 'I'm told he actually put a desk and a chair in the bar and said that Montgomery had used them. Apparently he also purloined an army officer's cap, put a red band on it and claimed that was Monty's, too.'

By the time Roy and his wife, Pauline, arrived in 1968, the legend had

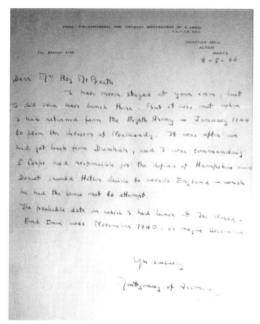

Monty's letter describing his visit in 1940

gathered even more ground. 'People were telling me how Eisenhower, Churchill, Montgomery and others were sitting on our lawn in 1944 planning the D-Day invasion,' Roy recalled. 'Just after I moved in one customer pointed at a chair in the corner of the bar and said: "That's the very chair he sat on, you know." I didn't have the heart to tell him I had just bought the chair in Wimborne for £8.' There were even picture postcards on the bar, which claimed that 'Monty planned the D-Day invasion here in 1942'.

The McBeaths decided to settle the matter by writing to Bernard Montgomery himself. They enclosed part of an Ordnance Survey map pinpointing the World's End and received a handwritten reply by return of post. The retired Field Marshal told them: 'I have never stayed at your inn but I did once have lunch there. But it was not when I had returned from the Eighth Army in January 1944 to plan the invasion of Normandy. It was after we had got back from Dunkirk and I was commanding 5 Corps and responsible for the defence of Hampshire and Dorset should Hitler decide to invade England – which he had the sense not to attempt. The probable date on which I had lunch at the World's End Inn was November 1940, or maybe December. Yours sincerely, Montgomery of Alamein.'

Although the letter appeared to kill off the D-Day story, it did at least confirm there was an element of truth in the legendary link with Monty. The McBeaths had the letter framed and hung on the wall – but still the legend persisted, with some customers unashamedly choosing to believe the romantic version in preference to Montgomery's own account.

The letter was thought to have perished in the fire but Roy McBeath later revealed that he had personally saved it before the fire took hold. When a rebuilt World's End rose from the ashes complete with thatch and timber beams and pillars, he restored it to its rightful place in the bar, where it remains to this day, hanging alongside many old photographs and militaria that have replaced the treasures that were lost.

The legend that the World's End had timbers salvaged from the Spanish Armada cannot be proved or disproved, as the structure was largely destroyed in the 1991 fire. But the Armada took place in 1589, which sits well with the belief that original building dated from the late sixteenth or early seventeenth century.

According to another legend, the World's End also holds the oldest beer licence in Dorset, though again there is no known proof. The building belonged to the Dashwood family in 1714 and records show that they held a licence for the premises in 1753. A document dated 1760 names the licensee as W. Cutler.

A report from Poole Customs House dated 1770 suggests that the World's End may once have been a favourite haunt of smugglers. The report describes how two Customs officers tracked a smuggling gang after hearing that forty heavily laden horses had passed over Holme Bridge, near Wareham. The hoof-prints led them to the World's End, where they found

The World's End today

a spread laid out for 'a great number of people'. The landlord refused to entertain the officers or stable their horses and they decided to split up and go for reinforcements. One headed for Blandford but failed to persuade a troop of dragoons stationed there to assist; the other went to Poole Customs House but officers took so long 'furnishing themselves with horses' that by the time they reached the World's End the smugglers had left and taken their contraband with them.

The pub is supposed to have housed a butcher's business in the early twentieth century. The World's End also held a licence for 'gilbert and baker', which gave it the right to stage auctions and bake bread. The bread oven next to the inglenook survived until the fire, as did a 'highwayman's bolthole', which ran parallel to the chimney and apparently provided a rapid escape route for anyone in trouble with the law.

CHAPTER THIRTY-ONE
The Charles Rolls Tragedy

Bournemouth has the dubious distinction of being the location of Britain's first fatal flying accident – and it happened during one of the biggest festivals in the seaside town's 206-year history. In fact, the Bournemouth Centenary Celebrations were brought to an abrupt albeit temporary halt by the tragedy that unfolded very publicly at Southbourne on 12 July 1910.

Bournemouth had organised a series of flying displays as part of a major programme of events marking 100 years since the Cranborne gentleman and Dorset Yeomanry officer Captain Lewis Tregonwell famously built a seaside mansion on the coastal heathland that is now the town centre. It was an example that thousands were to follow over the next few decades, earning Tregonwell the informal title of 'founder of Bournemouth'.

A century after Tregonwell's historic building project, flying was still in its infancy. Bournemouth had been given its first glimpse of powered flight only two months before the Centenary Celebrations when William E. McArdle and the American aviator J. A. Drexel organised a display from fields near Vine's Farm, Wallisdown.

The centenary displays were a much bigger affair, run over several days. They were effectively Britain's first international aviation meeting and the Burlington Hotel at Boscombe became the Royal Aero Club's temporary headquarters. Many pioneer aviators converged on Bournemouth to show

Charles Rolls at Southbourne in 1910.
Picture: National Motor Museum

off their courage and skill, including Colonel Samuel Franklin Cody, already famous as the first man to fly in Great Britain. Cody was born in America in 1861 but became a naturalised British subject. He was eventually to die in a flying accident in 1913.

The centenary displays took place at the brand new Bournemouth Aerodrome, which had been specially laid out on a mile of grassland between Tuckton and

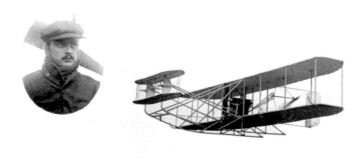

Charles Rolls (inset) and his ill-fated biplane before the fatal crash

Double Dykes at Southbourne. Grandstands and enclosures were built to accommodate thousands of spectators, who paid admission charges ranging from 2 shillings (10p) to £1.

On 12 July the events included a flying competition in which the aim was to land as near as possible to a designated spot. There had already been two crashes at the aerodrome that day but both pilots had escaped injury. The competitors for the landing competition included a pioneer of both motoring and aviation, the Honourable Charles Rolls, son of Lord Llangattock, a director of Rolls Royce and only the second man in England to fly a circular mile. Just after 1pm Rolls took off to make his second attempt at a prize-winning landing. His flight began well and to start with there was 'nothing to suggest he was about to make his last journey', reported the *Bournemouth Daily Echo* later that afternoon. The paper continued: 'His Short-Wright biplane rose majestically in the air and gracefully skirted the pylons that marked the inner corners of the course. Very quickly he rose to an altitude of 100 feet and on the return journey flew out of the course over the grandstand for a long volplane glide to the chalked circle in which he had to alight.'

What happened next prompted a 'horrified gasp' from the large crowd. 'He had cleared the stand and started on his descent when a sharp metallic snap was heard,' reported the *Echo*. 'Simultaneously some woodwork fell from the tail-end of the machine and a cry of horror went up when it was seen that the machine had lost its balance 60 or 70 feet in the air. There was a quiver of the huge framework and the whole structure dropped like a wounded bird.'

As the biplane broke up and plunged nose-first towards the ground, the 'horrified gasp' gave way to a 'terrified and breathless silence and then a scream of horror as the crash came'. Women fainted and men turned away in horror. 'It fell to the ground with a sickening crash heard all over the ground. In that instant the machine was reduced to scrap,' said the *Echo*. 'A wild rush was made to the scene by doctors, police and officials, and the crowd surged towards the wreckage eager to learn how the aviator had fared. Mr Rolls was gently lifted from the debris and all that human skill could accomplish was done. There was only a feeble glimmer of life, a faint tremble of the heart for the doctors to work to and in less than a minute all was over. The doctors announced that Mr Rolls had been killed instantaneously.'

The cause of death was a broken neck and a fracture at the base of the skull. The following day an inquest jury returned a verdict of death by misadventure.

Although the flying displays were abandoned for the day, they resumed the following day, as Mrs Nora Cooper, of St Leonards, near Ringwood, recalled in 1988. 'I was a little girl in 1910,' she told me, 'and I remember walking from Parkstone on the day of the tragedy and hearing people say, "Rolls is dead. Rolls is dead. The flying is cancelled." But we went again the next day and watched in awe. The planes just skimmed over the trees and we thought it was the most wonderful sight.'

Hangars at Southbourne showing Rolls' shed (left) closed up following his death.
Picture: National Motor Museum

Another milestone in Bournemouth's aviation history occurred in 1912, when Henri Farman landed his hydroplane near the Pier during a travelling display sponsored by the *Daily Mail*. The following year Gustav-Hamel established a looping record above Meyrick Park while at Pokesdown Henri Salmet gave six passenger flights before crashing into a tree.

In 1919, an aerodrome opened at Ensbury Park, offering commercial flights and occasional aeroplane races until an accident in 1927 in which three people died. Speaking seventy years later, Mr N. J. Pike recalled that the price of a circuit and landing in a small biplane was 5 shillings (25p) while 12s 6d (62.5p) would buy a trip around Poole Bay in a small twin-engined airliner. For the then princely sum of 30 shillings (£1.50) you could experience a power-dive in a red and silver monoplane.

The Ensbury Park aerodrome also hosted National Hunt racing in the mid to late 1920s. Mr Pike remembered watching it from his sister's home in Redhill Drive. 'We could watch the horse racing from the bedroom window,' he said. 'I was told later that a racehorse called Brown Jack had been sold there as a three-year-old for £300. It was subsequently raced at Ascot and won the longest distance race on the card, the Queen Alexandra Stakes, five years in succession.'

In fact Brown Jack won the Queen Alexandra six years running (1929-34) as well as the Ascot Stakes and Cheltenham Champion Hurdle in 1928, the Goodwood Cup and the Doncaster Cup in 1930 and the Chester Cup and the Ebor Handicap in 1931. The legendary thoroughbred even had a biography written about him and a bronze statue erected at Ascot, where the Brown Jack Stakes still feature in the programme nearly ninety years later.

By the early 1930s the former Ensbury Park aerodrome and racecourse was being redeveloped as housing with the first houses selling for £475. They are now priced in the hundreds of thousands of pounds.

CHAPTER THIRTY-TWO
The Legend of Lodge Farm

On the face of it, the story told to Steve Burden when he moved into his new home near Wimborne in 1977 was arrant nonsense. After telling the new tenant that he 'must be mad' to take on the abandoned farmhouse at the southern end of the famous Badbury Rings avenue of beech trees, the farmworkers across the garden fence shared a local legend. 'They told me that according to legend, the whole of England was once governed from here,' said Steve. 'To which I replied, "Yes, and I expect Henry VIII slept here as well".'

Forty years on there is reason to believe that the farmworkers' claim for the outwardly modest building should not be so readily dismissed after all. 'When I moved in, it had been abandoned for a few years, occupied by squatters for a while,' he said. 'It was derelict and totally overgrown and it took me a couple of days just to cut a path into the place.'

At the time of Steve's arrival, Lodge Farm at Kingston Lacy was officially recorded as a converted tithe barn with windows that had been removed from the lost church of nearby Pamphill. But as he stripped off wallpaper in the bedroom upstairs, Steve started to discover hidden fireplaces and blocked off windows. Whatever his house might have been in its early days, it clearly wasn't a barn.

Today Lodge Farm is recognised as one of the finest examples of a medieval hall house and the only surviving example in Dorset. There is also evidence that it was built on top of an earlier hunting lodge. 'The earlier building was pulled down when this one was built and the debris barrowed in to fill up the defensive ditches,' said Steve. 'It was also larger than the present building but just how large we don't yet know.'

Archaeology has produced finds from many eras, including knives, arrowheads and high quality pottery from the medieval period. Manorial records refer to a hunting lodge that stood in the midst of a 300-acre deer park at Badbury and Kingston Lacy.

It seems very likely that it was built by one of the Dukes of Lancaster, who owned a third of England in the late fourteenth century, including Kingston Lacy. The first Duke of Lancaster was John of Gaunt (1340-99), a son of Edward III, uncle of Richard II and father of Henry IV. He ruled as

Lodge Farm, Kingston Lacy

regent during his father's illness and is known to have visited Kingston Lacy, as his signature appears on a marriage proxy there. It was also the custom in those days for government officials to follow the King as he travelled around the country – which could perhaps explain the legend that England was once governed from here.

What Steve finds even more convincing are the building's defensive characteristics. 'The evidence for the John of Gaunt connection is circumstantial but the house was certainly built by someone with wealth and taste,' he said. 'The old-fashioned, defensive nature of the building – including the hall on the first floor – could reflect the troubled times of Richard II. John of Gaunt is recorded as having built semi-defensive hunting lodges on his estates. He was a very controversial figure, very unpopular. During the peasant's uprising of 1381, his stewards and houses were usually the first to be attacked.

'It's also a timber-framed building inside a stone and tiled cladding. Normally you would build frames and fill them with wattle and daub. The cost of building a three-feet-thick wall would have been prohibitive to most people. The quality of the work is outstanding. The building wasn't thrown together by some farm labourer or your average rabbit warrener, as has been suggested. It was built by skilled craftsmen. The floorboards between the floors are tongue-and-grooved, not just butt-jointed, and the screen between the solar and the great hall is a masterpiece of English joinery. The medieval timberwork has required no repairs at all after 600 years.'

As Steve stripped off wallpaper and plaster, he uncovered further evidence of the building's former grandeur, including wall paintings featuring bold and vivid patterns. Scratched on to one area of fourteenth-century plaster are two human figures, one possibly holding a spear. Upstairs one of the fireplaces is scarred by daggers sharpened on the stonework, while the wood partition between the grand hall and the solar or owner's private room bears the burn marks of candles which had been stuck into makeshift holders of clay slapped onto the wall. The iron-glazed first-floor windows were narrow, single-light ones, another defensive feature.

Documents from the Kingston Lacy Estate archives dated September 1380 record payments of 4d (2p) for 'cleaning of the lord's council' and 6d (2.5p) for 'straw purchased for bedding both in the chambers and in the stable for the same time'. New goblets, dishes and platters were also bought 'for those coming to the council'.

'They were obviously men of some importance,' said Stephen. 'This period in English history is known as the time of the "continual councils" as in 1380 King Richard II was just thirteen. If this was the council that ruled England, one of its last meetings must have been at Kingston Lacy, for in 1380 the "continual councils" were ended at the request of the Commons.'

The earliest probable written evidence of Lodge Farm comes from the manorial accounts, which refer to repairs carried out to the door in 1391. It was probably abandoned during the following century, perhaps after the death of Lord of the Manor, John Beaufort, in 1444. 'His death was rumoured to be suicide and an archaeologist has suggested that this, being a bad omen, may have led to the abandonment. The house had certainly fallen into decay by 1465,' said Steve.

By the seventeenth century, the house was occupied by people of a lower social class than those for whom it was intended. A brick lean-to was added around this time and a large bread oven and chimney probably in the late nineteenth century. At some stage the original medieval garderobe tower or privy was demolished.

Robert Short and John Sebery alias Roper were the tenants in 1636, when they held the 'Lodge and Warren of Badbury with a stock of 2000 couple of conies [4000 rabbits]'. The rabbit warren appears to have been a living goldmine, as each pair of conies was valued at 12d (5p). In 1668 William Short 'of Badbury Lodge' was reported for the offence of living in sin – or, in the words of the time, for 'the fame of living viciously and incontinently with Joan Cork, alias Short, his wife, before the solemnisation of matrimony'. He was ordered to purge himself publicly at Wimborne Minster.

Seventeenth-century finds include much local pottery, clay pipes and other domestic items and a mould for a William III one shilling coin, suggesting that there may have been counterfeiters in residence.

The site has proved rich in history from all periods. The old Roman road from Hamworthy to Badbury Rings runs through the garden and the camber can be clearly seen. There is evidence of a 500 BC Iron Age settlement on the site and nearby a dig connected with the BP pipeline project produced 4000-year-old neolithic pits, pottery, bone and flint implements.

CHAPTER THIRTY-THREE
The Real Poole Pirate

Mention 'Poole Pirates' today and most locals will think of the harbour town's successful speedway team. But Poole has had its share of real pirates too, including one of the best in the business. One Spanish scribe described Harry Pay as a 'knight who scours the seas as a corsair with many ships, plundering all the Spanish and French vessels that he can encounter'. He was also called 'the most implacable of the enemies of the French'.

From an English perspective, Pay was known for his valour and enterprise, for his defeat of the French in battle, for his help in suppressing a Welsh revolt and for his regular plundering of enemy vessels – work that was encouraged by king and government. At one point Pay was charged in England with piracy after seizing a cargo of wine from a French barque. But within a year he had been officially authorised to fit out privateers for the specific purpose of harassing the French.

According to tradition, Harry Pay was born in a house at the corner of Carter's Lane and Hill Street, Poole, in the latter half of the fourteenth century. Little is known of his early life but from the beginning of the fifteenth century his name appears regularly in official documents, usually as a result of complaints from foreign shores. In an era when cross-Channel relations were strained at best, he became a thorn in the side of the French and Spanish, who referred to him as 'Arripay'. The aforementioned Spanish chronicler wrote: 'This Arripay came often upon the coast of Castile and carried away many ships and vessels; and he scoured the Channel by Flanders so powerfully that no vessel could pass that way without being taken. This Arripay burnt Gijon and Finisterre and carried off the crucifix from Santa Maria de Finisterre, which was famous for being the holiest in those parts. Much more damage Arripay did in Castile, taking many prizes and exacting ransoms. Although other armed ships came there from England in like manner, he it was who came most often.'

Pay was one of the captains of an English fleet that burnt forty towns and villages in Normandy in 1405. Closer to home, in 1402 he boarded the *Marie* from Bilbao off the Isle of Wight and seized a glittering cargo of gold, silver and expensive clothes. Those of the Spanish crew who survived the initial onslaught were mercilessly beaten before being set adrift in an open boat towards the French coast. Pay's ruthlessness was to have repercussions for Poole. In 1405, furious about these and other attacks, a squadron of five Spanish galleys, supported by two smaller French ships, singled out Pay's home port for special treatment during a mission to harass England's south coast. Those on board included a large contingent of crossbowmen.

According to the Spanish account of this raid, the flotilla entered Poole Harbour at dawn and discovered that the town was 'not walled and there was a fine tower with a cupola' (the original St James's church). The French commander deemed it unwise to attempt a landing but the Spanish leader, Don Pero Nino, believing his country's honour to be at stake, sent in a raiding party with orders to set fire to the houses but not to burden themselves with plunder. This was plain vengeance.

The dawn attack, led by Pero Nino's cousin, Fernando Nino, took Poole by surprise and it was some time before the townsfolk were able to organise their archers and men-at-arms. Removing the doors of their homes to use as shields against the crossbow bolts, they put up a stern defence of their town. Many on both sides were wounded and those Spaniards protected by armour were said to have been 'fledged with arrows' fired by the Poole longbowmen. The showers of arrows raining down on the Spaniards were so thick that the crossbowmen were unable to stoop to draw their bows.

The Spanish retreated three paces and brought in reinforcements, led by Pero Nino himself. Amid cries of 'Santiago! Santiago!' – literally 'St James! St James!', who ironically is the patron saint of Poole as well as of Spain – the Spanish and French troops forced the defenders to retreat. The attack caused such devastation that it took many years for Poole to recover its commercial importance. Harry Pay himself was away on pirate's business and missed it all. By another irony, his home was among the few houses to escape the raging fire but his brother was among those killed.

Undeterred, Pay pulled off the most audacious of his many exploits just a year later. The prince of pirates appeared to have met his match when his ship was boarded by crewmen from a Normandy man-of-war during a short-lived truce in 1406. After a desperate hand-to-hand battle, Pay and his men were forced to surrender and tied up with ropes to await their deaths. Their captors then removed their protective helmets, gauntlets and armour and went below deck to assess the cargo, leaving two men to guard the English pirates. Pretending to make final confessions of their sins to each other, Pay and his boys used the conversation to plan their escape. Overpowering the guards and seizing their weapons, they then despatched the rest of the Normans as they emerged from the hold.

At this point any other captain would have looted the French ship before scuttling her and sailing for home. But this was Harry Pay and he had more ambitious plans. Instead of destroying the opposing ship, he took her over, posing as her master and sailing her under the French flag with his own vessel in tow. He even persuaded another English rover to join the enterprise, then sailed up the River Seine posing as a Frenchman returning home triumphantly with his two English prizes.

This time it was the turn of the French to be taken by surprise. Finding themselves alongside numerous French ships moored on the river, Pay and friends embarked on an unprecedented spree of looting and burning, took all that they wanted and returned to the Channel unscathed.

While the 1406 Seine adventure saw Pay at his most audacious, his most successful expedition in terms of plunder was in 1407, when he brought home no fewer than 120 vessels laden with iron, salt and oil, all captured off the Brittany coast.

But the line between piracy and officialdom was a fine one and later references suggest that Pay's talents were increasingly embraced by those in power. A leading historian of piracy and smuggling, the late Dr Neville Williams, whose job as Assistant Director of the Public Record Office gave him unique access to medieval documents, says Pay later served in Thomas Berkeley's squadron 'for keeping the seas against pirates' – a classic case of poacher-turned-gamekeeper. 'When he was too old for service afloat, a grateful government found an appropriate niche for him and he ended his days full of honour as water bailiff at Calais,' adds Williams.

Harry Pay died on 25 March 1419 and was buried in the church of St Mary of Charity at Faversham, Kent, where the remains of a memorial brass can still be seen. Most of the brass effigy has long since been torn away but the feet and footplate and part of the inscription survive and it is clear that the figure was originally depicted wearing chain and plate armour of the period.

CHAPTER THIRTY-FOUR
The Bloody Assize

Few stories from Dorset's past are more laden with drama than the sequence of events that began at Lyme Regis on a June evening in 1685. And it was a sequence that was to have major national as well as local implications.

It was at dusk on 11 June that James Duke of Monmouth landed at the West Dorset port accompanied by eighty armed supporters. The eldest of King Charles II's illegitimate children and was staunchly Protestant – unlike the other claimant to the throne, the dead King's Catholic brother James II. Monmouth chose Lyme Regis for his landing as the area had many Dissenters, who were known for their strong anti-Catholic feelings.

Over the next three weeks, more than 3000 supporters rallied to his side, including a third of Lyme Regis's adult male population. But at the decisive Battle of Sedgemoor in Somerset on 6 July, the Duke's little army of rural warriors was soundly beaten by the King's troops.

Monmouth re-entered Dorset as a fugitive with a £5000 reward on his head. He was hoping to reach Poole and from there to escape to Holland. At Woodyates, between Blandford and Salisbury, he disguised himself as a shepherd. But at Horton Heath, near the modern town of Verwood (then a scattered village called Fairwood), Monmouth and a companion were spotted by an elderly woman as they climbed over a hedge. The woman had an eye for a reward and informed the troops who were already searching nearby.

The Duke was found on 8 July sleeping rough under an ash tree.

James Duke of Monmouth

Judge Jeffreys gives his name to a Dorchester restaurant

He was arrested and taken across the Dorset-Hampshire border to Ringwood, where he wrote a letter of remorse to his uncle. The King, however, was in no mood to be merciful and Monmouth was publicly beheaded on Tower Hill by an incompetent executioner, who needed seven blows to complete his terrible task.

But this was only half the story. The other half concerns the brutal backlash that followed. A few weeks after Monmouth's ill-fated attempt to seize the throne, James II dispatched Judge George Jeffreys to the West Country to deal with the hundreds who stood accused of involvement in the rebellion. The Lord Chief Justice wasted no time in making his intentions clear. At Winchester he made outrageous directions to the jury on both law and fact during the trial of Dame Alice Lisle, of Moyle's Court, near Ringwood, who was charged with harbouring two of the rebels. Then he sentenced the seventy-year-old to be burnt at the stake, although in the end the sentence was commuted to the more instant beheading following a plea to the King.

At Dorchester on 5 September, Judge Jeffreys ordered his courtroom at the Antelope Hotel in Dorchester to be hung with red cloth before opening the proceedings. Then, in the words of one writer, he 'bullied witnesses and counsel alike; guilt was predetermined. Often he foamed at the mouth in his frenzy.'

Jeffreys dealt with thirty defendants on the first morning, sentencing twenty-nine to be hanged, drawn and quartered. By the end of the week, 312 people had appeared before him, of whom seventy-four were to be executed, 175 transported and nine fined or whipped or both.

Among those sentenced to death at Dorchester was the parish constable of Chardstock, Thomas Smith, who enraged Jeffreys by advising the jury that they should give little credence to the evidence, since the witnesses against him were the same as those against his neighbour, Matthew Bragg.

'Thou villain! Methinks I see thee already with a halter about thy neck,' bawled the judge. 'Thou impudent rebel! To challenge the King's evidence!'

He ordered that Smith be the first to die in the Dorchester executions, which he was.

Matthew Bragg was a lawyer who attended the court in his professional capacity but found himself in the dock accused of pointing out the home of a Roman Catholic priest to a group of Monmouth's men, who 'obliged him to do so'. Like Smith and eleven others, he was executed at Dorchester on 7 September.

There was worse to come. At the Assizes for Somerset and Devon, the total number sentenced by Jeffreys to execution reached 331. A further 850 were to be sold as slaves in the King's plantations in America and 408 faced fines, whippings, imprisonment or other forms of punishment. Two of those

Judge Jeffreys

sentenced to death were executed immediately for pleading not guilty in defiance of the judge's directions.

Most of Jeffreys' victims were ordinary West Country folk – 'shopkeepers, tailors, mariners, weavers, shoemakers, poor common men and lads and even boys'. In many cases the evidence against them was weak or dubious; some were clearly innocent. One man faced execution for accepting the Duke of Monmouth's handshake as he rode through his village. Another went to the gallows in lieu of his brother, who had escaped arrest.

At Lyme Regis, a young woman sank to her knees and begged that her fiancé be spared, to which Judge Jeffreys replied that he could spare only part of him, and as he knew which part she liked best, he would give orders to the sheriff accordingly. Among the others executed at Lyme was a 'very old man', who was supported by the parish. When told this, the judge declared that they had no occasion to trouble themselves on that account, for he would relieve them of the charge.

The ruthless Jeffreys even managed to line his pockets through his work, selling pardons to those who could pay and taking commission on those sold into slavery. One girl clung to the wheels of his carriage, weeping and begging the judge to permit the release her executed brother's remains so it could be buried in consecrated ground. Jeffreys accepted a fee of £1000 for the return of the body.

In a few days Jeffreys had become the most notorious judge in British history – a man whose very name sent shivers down the spines of generations in Dorset and Somerset. King James II took a different view, rewarding Judge Jeffreys for his work by promoting him to Lord Chancellor. But time was running out for the Catholic cause and when the Protestant William of Orange landed in 1688, Jeffreys was reduced to disguising himself as a seaman and taking refuge in Wapping, London. He was eventually recognised, however, and removed to the Tower of London, where he died on 18 April 1689, aged forty-one.

CHAPTER THIRTY-FIVE

A Dorset Family's Place in History

When four adults and four children left Sturminster Newton in the summer of 1792, they knew they were going on the adventure of a lifetime – an adventure laden with challenges and from which they would probably never return. What Thomas and Jane Rose, their children, their niece and their dairymaid could not have known is that their courage would earn them a unique place in history which would still be remembered and celebrated more than two centuries later. They were about to become the first 'free settlers' on the continent of Australia.

The family were among just fourteen people who responded to a Government appeal for experienced farmers and 'other right kind of settler' to become pioneers in Britain's newest overseas colony. The first Governor of New South Wales, Captain Arthur Philip, realised that if the penal colony were to develop in a balanced and productive way, he needed something more than convicts who had been sentenced to transportation and their guards.

The Government offered various incentives, including a free passage to the other side of the world, land, tools and implements and enough provisions to last two years and clothing for one year. Convict labour would also be available. But this was not a project for the faint-hearted. It involved a five-month voyage across the world's great oceans, all the challenges of an alien environment and climate and the likelihood that you would never see your family, friends and former home again. Which may be why only fourteen volunteers – or more accurately fifteen – were on board the supply ship *Bellona* when she sailed from Gravesend on 8 August 1792.

The Sturminster Newton contingent were the only complete family group among the voluntary settlers. Embarking with farmers Thomas and Jane Rose, aged forty-one and thirty-three and previously of Puxey Farm, were their children Thomas, who was thirteen, eleven-year-old Mary, Joshua, aged nine, and two-year-old Richard. Also on the *Bellona* were the couple's niece, Elizabeth Fish, and the Roses' dairymaid, Elizabeth Watts. Most accounts give the ages of both Elizabeths as eighteen but a little-known

Puxey Farm, Sturminster Newton, former home of the Rose family

medical report from Rio de Janeiro, where the *Bellona* broke her voyage on 24 October 1792, gives Elizabeth Fish's age as twenty-four. The report from Brazil also provides another surprise – that Elizabeth Fish had a baby daughter, who had died nine days into the voyage due to 'worm fever and convulsions'. The child's age is given as one.

The other six voluntary migrants were all men from other parts of the country, four of whom had already been to New South Wales as seamen so at least knew what they had in store. They were baker Frederick Meredith, who was twenty-eight; master blacksmith Walter Brodie, thirty-three; millwright James Thorpe, forty-seven, who was to be paid a salary of £100 a year for using his skills; Edward Powell, thirty-one, described as a 'farmer and fisherman' from Lancaster; gardener Thomas Webb, thirty-four; and his nephew, Joseph Webb, twenty-one, a farmer.

The voyage was not all plain sailing. As well as the baby's death, the infant Richard Rose also suffered from worm fever and convulsions but survived while his mother was described at one point as being of 'indifferent health'. Many of the seventeen women convicts who also sailed on the *Bellona* suffered from fevers and scurvy. A large proportion of the supplies destined for both the convict community and the settlers also failed to survive the journey. Sixty-nine casks of flour were described upon arrival

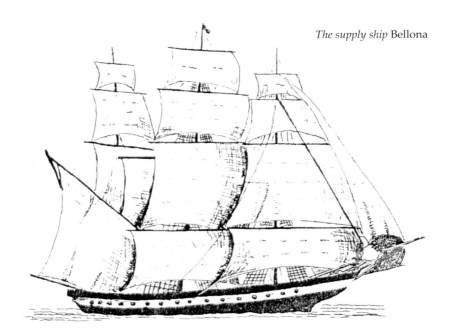

The supply ship Bellona

as 'rotten, stinking and maggotty' due to damp; pork was 'stinking, rotten and unfit to eat'; hundreds of gallons of rum and wine and almost 1200 gallons of molasses had dribbled away due to leaks; huge quantities of cloth, hammocks and rugs were 'rotten and decayed from a continuance of wet on the passage out'; and a case of stationery was 'totally damaged and unfit for use'.

The voyage was also eventful in other ways. Jane Rose fell pregnant during the voyage and gave birth to her fifth child, John, six months after the *Bellona's* arrival at Sydney Cove on 16 January 1793. Edward Powell and Elizabeth Fish struck up a relationship while at sea and married not long after their arrival. Romance also blossomed for Thomas Webb and Catherine Buckley, one of the women convicts, and they married eight days after reaching Australia. A little over two years later, however, Buckley became a widow after Webb was fatally speared by aborigines. By this time his nephew had also died.

Thomas Rose was allocated 120 acres on arrival in Australia followed by a further 70 acres in 1798 as a reward for his industry. The family chose to set up home 7 miles west of Sydney at a place they called Liberty Plains, later the Strathfield-Homebush district. There is a suggestion that Rose was under pressure from Lieutenant Governor Francis Grose to choose the site, as Grose was keen to establish a settlement between Sydney and Parramatta 'for the safety and convenience of the travelling public'. Rose later concluded he had made a 'hasty and bad choice of situation'. The soil was poor and there was little or no manure or fertiliser to improve it. The Roses faced crop failures and water shortages and also survived an aboriginal attack during which Jane was hit by a spear and saved only by her whalebone corset.

Family records suggest that Rose moved his family to Prospect, where he was made an overseer in charge of the Government farm and stock. Jane also gave birth to her sixth and seventh children, Sarah and Henry. In the early 1800s the Roses moved again to more fertile land on the north bank of the Hawkesbury River at Wilberforce not far from Sydney. Here Thomas became a well-known and highly respected figure. One account describes him as 'quiet, homely, unassuming and industrious'.

After having several bark shelters and huts wrecked by floods as well as crops and livestock destroyed, the family built a sturdier log cabin on higher ground. The house was built of split iron-bark slabs to make it resistant to native white ants. The rafters and floor were pit-sawn with wattle and cow manure daubed on the inside walls to provide a smooth surface free of cracks and gaps. The wattle and daub was later replaced with a lining of pine boards.

Rose Cottage, as the house is known, originally comprised a large living room, kitchen and two bedrooms. It was altered and extended over the years but amazingly remained in the Rose family until 1961. Today it survives as a tourist attraction – the oldest timber house in Australia and part of the Wilberforce Australiana Pioneer Village. It is managed by the Thomas and Jane Rose Society.

The Roses, meanwhile, took their duties of populating the colony very seriously. By the time of Jane Rose's death in 1827, she had become Australia's first non-aboriginal great-grandmother with more than 100 descendants. Her husband died six years later aged eighty-four. By the late twentieth century, the number of known descendants of Jane (née Topp) and Thomas Rose had risen to almost 27,600 although the true number is thought to be over 60,000.

From a letter sent to Jane by her parents Thomas and Mary Topp of Sturminster Newton in 1798, we can glimpse the England that they had left behind. This was at a time when Napoleon was riding roughshod over Europe and threatening to add Britain to his conquests while taxes were rising rapidly to pay for the wars with France. 'The times in England are very hazardous and everything is very dear,' says the letter, held by the State Library of New South Wales. 'And every week threatened with an invasion

Artist's impression of Rose Cottage as it would have looked in the early 1800s

Rose Cottage in the twentieth century Photo: Sturminster Newton Museum

by the French, and we believe it will surely be so, as they are fully intended to invade this country.'

The Topps speak of taxes so heavy that they were 'hardly to be borne'. These included 'a tax upon saddle horses three guineas a year; 16 shillings 'pon each cart horse; clocks and watches; stamps 'pon gloves and hats; butter now 11d per pound; beef (good) 6d pound; ordinary cheese £1 10s per hundredweight; a hard tax 'pon dogs. They talk 'pon taxing the cows and many other taxes too tedious to mention.'

The invasion threat also meant that military movements were much in evidence. 'We have now horses and men called yeoman cavalry and another sort called provisional cavalry, for the defence of the nation. There are talks of several large camps this year.'

Jane and Thomas Rose's tens of thousands of direct descendants included Louisa Prince (née Rose), who marked the 200th anniversary of the *Bellona*'s departure by visiting her ancestors' Dorset home. On 8 August 1992, 200 years to the day after embarkation, the seventy-two-year-old Mrs Prince was one of three Australian descendants at a garden party at *Puxey Farm*, Sturminster Newton, which the Roses had farmed before setting sail. On the same day she attended a 'gala opening' of a small exhibition on the Roses at Sturminster Newton Museum.

In January 1993, hundreds of Rose descendants were among 2000 people who headed for Sydney Cove, Australia, to celebrate the 200th anniversary of the *Bellona*'s arrival Down Under with the first 'free settlers'. Some descendants donned period costume to re-enact the historic landing by their forebears. The celebrations also included a '*Bellona* muster' involving descendants of both settlers and female convicts and a flag-raising ceremony. A beacon was also lit as happened two centuries earlier to warn the *Bellona*'s crew of the hazards of entering the harbour after dark.

Principal Sources

The Skeleton in Mary's Cupboard
Roger Guttridge, 'The Skeleton in Mary's Cupboard', *Stour and Avon Magazine*, 5 February 2010, p41
Cuttings in the Priest's House Museum Library

Puddletown's Royal Secret
Roger Guttridge, 'Dorset's Role in Royal Scandal', *Wimborne Community Magazines*, 27 January 2005, p36
Lucille Iremonger, Love and the Princess (1958)

The Execution of Martha Brown
Roger Guttridge, *Dorset Murders* (Wimborne, 1986)
Nichola Thorne, *In Search of Martha Brown* (Sturminster Newton, 2000)
Nichola Thorne, *My Name is Martha Brown* (2000)

The War That Destroyed a Family
Roger Guttridge, 'The War That Destroyed a Family', *Blackmore Vale Magazine* 17 December 2004, p38

The Boscombe Whale
Roger Guttridge, 'A Whale of a Tale is Found', *Daily Echo* (Bournemouth), 17 April 1997, p17
Roger Guttridge, 'A Whale of a Laugh at the Concert', *Daily Echo* (Bournemouth), 24 April 1997, p11
Roger Guttridge, 'The Boscombe Whale', *Dorset Life*, No. 256 (2000), p42

Hutchins' Unsung Heroine
Terence Davis, *Wareham: Gateway to Purbeck* (Sherborne, 1984)

Churchill's Bridge Too Far
Roger Guttridge, *The Evening Echo Book of Heritage in Dorset and the New Forest* (Southampton, 1991)
Roger Guttridge, 'Fighting Them on the Bridges', *Wimborne Community Magazines*, 10 October 2002, p21

The Coffin in the Crypt
F. Fane, 'A Legend of Milton', *Proceedings of the Dorset Natural History and Antiquarian Field Club* vol xvi (Dorchester, 1895)
Roger Guttridge, *Ten Dorset Mysteries* (Southampton, 1989)
Westminster Abbey Muniment Room and Library, Inquest Papers into John Damer's death (1776)
Maria L. White, Westminster Inquests (unpublished, Westminster Abbey Muniment Room and Library, 1980)

The Shapwick Express
Roger Guttridge, 'Dorset's First Olympian', *Community Magazines*, 6 July 2000, p51
Roger Guttridge, 'A Legend in his Lifetime', *Blackmore Vale Magazine*, 27 July 2012, p43

The Lecherous Squire of Woodlands
Roger Guttridge, 'Tale of a Noted Squire', *Daily Echo* (Bournemouth), 20 November 1997, p22
Roger Guttridge, 'The Lecherous Squire of Woodlands', *Community Magazines*, 1 June 2000, p36
Roger Guttridge, 'A Dorset Life For Me', *Dorset Life*, February 2016 (2016), p98

The Reformed Highwayman
Roger Guttridge, *The Evening Echo Book of Heritage in Dorset and the New Forest* (Southampton, 1991)
Roger Guttridge, 'Highwayman John Became a Celebrity', Daily Echo (Bournemouth), 7 October 1993, p14
John Pafford, John Clavell 1601-43: Highwayman, Author, Lawyer, Doctor (Oxford, 1993)

The Durweston Poltergeist
Paul Joire, *Psychical and Supernormal Phenomena, Their Observation and Experimentation* (1916)
Roger Guttridge, *Ten Dorset Mysteries* (Southampton, 1989)
Roger Guttridge, *Paranormal Dorset* (Stroud, 2009)

The Runaway Rector
Author's interview with the late Pete Sherry of Maperton
Julietta Forrester, Diaries (unpublished, 1856-1917)
Roger Guttridge, 'The Runaway Vicar', *Blackmore Vale Magazine*, 29 June 2012, p58
Roger Guttridge, 'The Runaway Rector (Part 2)', *Blackmore Vale Magazine*, 17 August 2012, p56

The Waterway That Never Was
Kenneth R. Clew, *The Dorset and Somerset Canal* (Newton Abbot, 1971)
Roger Guttridge, *The Evening Echo Book of Heritage in Dorset and the New Forest* (Southampton, 1991)

The Tuckton Tolstoyans
Author's correspondence with Annika Tallo of Tallin, Estonia, Roger Guttridge, *The Evening Echo Book of Heritage in Dorset and the New Forest* (Southampton, 1991)
Roger Guttridge, 'When Revolution Came to Town', *Daily Echo* (Bournemouth), 6 March 1997, p24

The Body in the Bank
Roger Guttridge, 'A Triple Tragedy', *Dorset Life*, December 1997
Theresa Murphy, *Murder in Dorset* (1988)

The Bettiscombe Skull
Rodney Legg, *Mysterious Dorset* (Sherborne, 1987)
John Symonds Udal, *Dorsetshire Folk-lore* (Exeter, 1989)

The Shapwick Monster
Roger Guttridge, *The Evening Echo Book of Heritage in Dorset and the New Forest* (Southampton, 1991)
Roger Guttridge, 'The Shapwick Monster', *Wimborne Community Magazines*, 10 April 2003, p45

She Who Sold Seashells
Crispin Tickell, *Mary Anning of Lyme Regis* (Lyme Regis, 1996)
Diana Trenchard, *Women of Dorset* (Tiverton, 1994)
Wikipedia (online)

Ferndown Zoo and Other Animals
Brian Davis, *Ferndown: The Back of Beyond* (Brentwood, 1996)
Roger Guttridge and Audrey Greenhalgh, *Ferndown: A Pictorial History* (Chichester, 1997)
Roger Guttridge, 'Bears, Naked Navvies and a Lost Fire Engine', *Dorset Life*, No. 283 (2002), p45

Stalbridge and the Father of Chemistry
Roger Guttridge, *Paranormal Dorset* (Stroud, 2009)
Roger Guttridge, 'Manor House Held Secret of Killing by Fire', *Evening Echo* (Bournemouth), 12 November 1992, p26
Irene Jones, *Robert Boyle: Lord of the Manor of Stalbridge* (Sturminster Newton, 1989)
Rodney Legg, *Literary Dorset* (Wincanton, 1990)
Rev. W. S. Swayne, *History and Antiquities of Stalbridge* (1889)

The Ghost in the Gallery
Dorset History Centre (DHC), 'A True Account of An Apparition in the County of Dorset', D/WLC/Z22
DHC, Notice of Cororner's Inquest into John Daniel's Death, D131/X8
Roger Guttridge, *Paranormal Dorset* (Stroud, 2009)
Roger Guttridge, *Ten Dorset Mysteries* (Southampton, 1989)
Rodney Legg, *Mysterious Dorset* (Sherborne, 1987)

Smugglers in the Church
J. Mead Falkner, *Moonfleet* (1898)
Roger Guttridge, *Dorset Smugglers* (Wincanton, 1984)
W. M. Hardy, *Smuggling Days in Purbeck* (Dorchester, 1907)
R. J. Saville, *A Langton Smuggler* (Langton Matravers, 1976)

The Sherborne Poisoner
J. D. Casswell, *A Lance for Liberty* (1961)
Roger Guttridge, *Dorset Murders* (1986)

The Other Father of Evolution
Roger Guttridge, *The Evening Echo Book of Heritage in Dorset and the New Forest* (Southampton, 1991)
Roger Guttridge, 'Dorset's Link with Fathers of Evolution', *Blackmore Vale Magazine*, 12 December 2002, p35
Roger Guttridge, 'The Man Who Could Have Been Darwin', *Stour and Avon Magazine*, 28 June 2013, p36

Farmer Jesty's 'Quantum Leap'
Sheilagh Hill, *The Book of Yetminster* (Tiverton, 2005)
Paul Hyland, *The Ingrained Island* (1978)
Rodney Legg, *Purbeck Island* (Wincanton 1972, 1989)
Patrick J. Pead, *Benjamin Jesty: Dorset's Vaccination Pioneer* (Chichester, 2009)

The Pulpit with Bullet Holes
John Fair and Don Moxom, *Abbotsbury and the Swannery* (Wimborne, 1993)
Tim Goodwin, *Dorset in the Civil War 1625-1665* (Tiverton, 1996)

Cromwell and the Clubmen
Tim Goodwin, *Dorset in the Civil War 1625-1665* (Tiverton, 1996)

Manston's Unique Place in History
Anthony Adolph, Cremation in Britain (website, 2012)
Julietta Forrester, Diaries (unpublished, 1856-1917)

Monty Dined Here
Roger Guttridge, *The Evening Echo Book of Heritage in Dorset and the New Forest* (Southampton, 1991)

The Charles Rolls Tragedy
Roger Guttridge, *The Evening Echo Book of Heritage in Dorset and the New Forest* (Southampton, 1991)

The Legend of Lodge Farm
Roger Guttridge, *The Evening Echo Book of Heritage in Dorset and the New Forest* (Southampton, 1991)
Conversations with Stephen Burden

The Real Poole Pirate
Cecil N. Cullingford, *A History of Poole* (Chichester, 1988; Bodmin, 2003)
Roger Guttridge, *The Evening Echo Book of Heritage in Dorset and the New Forest* (Southampton, 1991)
David Mitchell, *Pirates* (1976)
Neville Williams, *Captains Outrageous: Seven Centuries of Piracy* (1961)

The Bloody Assize
Cecil N. Cullingford, *A History of Dorset* (Chichester, 1980)
Roger Guttridge, *The Evening Echo Book of Heritage in Dorset and the New Forest* (Southampton, 1991)

A Dorset Family's Place in History
Roger Guttridge, 'First Free Settlers were from Dorset', *Evening Echo* (Bournemouth), 6 August 1992, p18
Roger Guttridge, 'Sturminster's Part in History of "Oz"', *Wimborne Community Magazines*, 20 June 2002, p20
Sturminster Newton Museum, Archived cuttings and documents
Kenneth R. Topp, 'Dorset and Australia 1788-1988', *Dorset Year Book* 1989